WALK WITH ME

Find How Postal Landmarks Define the Lore, Traditions and Society of Mathews County, Virginia

Catherine C. Brooks

ISBN 0-7414-2603-X

Published by:
INFINITY
PUBLISHING.COM
1094 New DeHaven Street, Suite 100
West Conshohocken, PA 19428-2713
Info@buybooksontheweb.com
www.buybooksontheweb.com
Toll-free (877) BUY BOOK
Local Phone (610) 941-9999
Fax (610) 941-9959

Printed in the United States of America

Printed on Recycled Paper

Published June 2005

Contents

Chapter Four

Chapter Five

Chapter Six

Dedication

To my Aunt Marguerite Richardson Sadler,
whose research made the book possible.

Acknowledgments

I have dedicated this book to my aunt, who spent most of the hot summer days of 1966 in the National Archives, Washington, D.C., acquiring the information that is the backbone for my book. Having the dates the post offices operated and postmasters who served Mathews County's 44 post offices gave a boost to my search.

I wish to thank Dr. Edwin (Ned) Logan, the Score Representative for Mathews County, who initiated the idea for this book. Many thanks to Elsa C. Verbyla, editor of the *Gloucester-Mathews Gazette-Journal,* who has been cooperative, allowing me to use information and pictures from the paper's archives. "Mathews County Historical Society" has been most helpful in permitting use of their publications and information in the Archives. I have used information from Polly Cary Mason's book, *Colonial Records of Gloucester County, Vol. II,* both *History and Progress* editions and other information as noted within the paragraphs I use it. Thanks to Reed Lawson, archivist for MCHS, for the hours she spent with me in Tompkins Cottage, pulling upstairs files for me to copy downstairs. After the files were stored in Mathews Library's Archives, Reed Lawson, Becky Barnhardt and Bonnie Smith have all been helpful; so more thanks. Norman Rohrer, instructor, author and copy editor, gave of his time, editing and guiding me to an interesting format. Peter J. Wrike, who allowed me to use information from his book, *The Governor's Island—* thanks. Thanks to my children, Wade and Susan, and John W. Dixon, who gave assistance with editing photographs.

Dixon spent time locating proper buildings that housed Gwynn P. O. Those, who have answered the requests Elsa Verbyla and I made in the *Gloucester-Mathews Gazette-Journal*, have added interest to dull facts. I've included every story given whether it is tradition or fact. Postmasters have been helpful with present information. Thanks to each for you wrote this book.

Map Courtesy of *Gloucester-Mathews Gazette-Journal*

The 44 post offices, past and present of Mathews County

Prologue

Take a "walk with me" back in time before paved roads, automobiles, telephones, radios, television, computers and electricity—those things we take for granted. Except for the Chiskoyack Indian tribes, who camped on the shores of what is now Mathews County's many waterways, cleared fields for corn and tobacco, made trails through the trees and underbrush to hunt, we would call the place a wilderness. The Chiskoyacks traveled waterways, using dugout canoes, taking them far from their birthplace. Young tribesmen found new sites to camp, brought their squaws and developed communities. They conveyed messages across distances with smoke signals because from the time God created man, he has found a need to communicate one with the other.

When 105 Englishmen landed at the place known today as Jamestown, Virginia, in May 1607, they had no need for post offices or mail carriers other than the little ships traveling to and from England. The King of England governed the colony so must keep in communication with his subjects, whom he sent in search of gold. As more Englishmen and women arrived, the colony expanded well beyond Jamestown Island. They traveled principally by boat for it proved the easiest means to reach the many peninsulas and islands. After the Englishmen found a river that they named "York," some of the men settled on both shores. In time they settled the peninsula north of the York and named it Gloucester. Then the officials divided it into parishes. In 1779 the largest parish, known as Kingston, lying on the eastern end of the county, seceded. The new county seat became Mathews County, named for General Thomas Mathews, who influenced permission to grant the signers of the petition for a new county seat for which they proved a need.

During the earlier years, the settlers in Virginia depended on boats or men on foot to deliver both correspondence and merchandise. After the Spaniards introduced horses from Mexico to what white men called the New World, men learned to utilize the animals for riding, carrying burdens, and pulling sleds and later vehicles. When they became available to the settlers, correspondence and merchandise traveled over land more efficiently.

Thirteen years after the landing at Jamestown, another English group landed further north at Plymouth in what today is Massachusetts. Knowledge of Postal Service in Europe motivated the colonists to action—pursuing the same. However, the northern colonies contended for postal delivery earlier than the Virginia Colony.

"The earliest record appeared in the General Court of Massachusetts in 1639 when a tavern of the certain Richard Fairbanks was—*appointed for all letters, which are brought from beyond the seas, or are to be sent thither, to be left with him, and he is to take care that they are delivered, or sent according to direction."* (Quote from *History of the United Postal Service 1775-1979 Web Site 2001)* European nation's coffee houses and taverns had served as mail drops until this time.

Nearly fifty years later, officials established a post in Virginia. But since before the mid 1600s, delivery and pick-up of written messages had traveled to and from Gloucester County (now Gloucester and Mathews Counties) by way of sailing schooners to one or more plantations in designated regions along the coast. Private messengers, usually slaves, connected the plantations with deliveries: a hogshead (a barrel of 63 pounds) of tobacco was the penalty for failing to relay mail to the next plantation. Other records prove letters and newspapers arrived at Henry Rispess's Tavern from Gloucester Court House before the post office became official. Therefore we can envision the way Mathews County's residents received most early correspondence.

The second to the smallest county in the state of Virginia, Mathews boasts 44 officially registered post offices. Remember, residents of the growing county fetched their mail on foot, by boat, and the more affluent with horse and carriage through the nineteenth century. We'll visit each of these locations, many of which are but history.

In order to assist the twenty-first century reader to know the location of the communities with post offices, I've given both route numbers and road names. Since the road names didn't become finalized until late 2004, they wouldn't be needed by the readers, who have lived in Mathews their lifetime. However, for new residents and our youth, they will be essential.

Chapter One

First Post Offices in Mathews County

"Neither snow nor rain nor heat nor gloom of night stays these carriers from swift completion of their appointed rounds." General Post Office, New York City, 8th Avenue and 33rd Street

Mathews County's earliest records reveal that the county had no official post office until nine years and four months after it seceded from Gloucester County. However, Polly Cary Mason recorded in her book *Colonial Records of Gloucester County*, Vol. II that in 1794 both James and Henry VanBibber received mail at the tavern of Henry Rispess (later spelt Respress) in Mathews Court House. They paid the mail carrier $1 each for their bundles, making one believe each received a large amount of letters and newspapers, or some suppose the transport was a very lucrative business. A dollar was a good sum in 1794. Perhaps the tavern had been a drop off place for mail since Rispess opened its doors. (Mason's book in MCHS archives)

In 1798, when John Adams was president, twenty-four leading citizens of Mathews signed a subscription paper, assuring delivery of mail to and from the county. Mr. Richard Billups received $35 a year to carry and fetch letters and newspapers to and from the Henry Rispess Tavern, which sat on Main Street in the area that Hudgins Pharmacy occupies today. Research from the United States Postal Service National Archives in Washington D.C. reveals Matthews Court House Post Office was established September 1, 1800, and Henry Rispess served as the first Postmaster.

Mathews Court House, or "Westville" as it had been known earlier, was located on a little creek putting in from East River, now known as Put-In Creek. The three original brick buildings, dating back to the early 1790s, and including the courthouse, old clerk's office and jail, stand on the court green today. Mathews Court House referred to both the county seat and principal business district of the county. In the 1800-era the village boasted 30 houses, four mercantile stores, one tan yard, three boot and shoe factories, one tailor, two blacksmiths, one saddler, one carriage maker and one tavern. The Court House also included the Court Building, clerk's office and two jails—one for criminals and the other for debtors. The population of the immediate town totaled 150, including three physicians. (The physicians treated both folks in the village and those in outlying areas.)

We assume that Rispess performed his tasks much as postmasters did a century later. When the latest batch of mail had been sorted, Rispess called the names of the recipients that appeared on the envelopes and bundles. Thus "mail call" became a daily practice. Each man, waiting for mail, stepped forward to receive his letters and newspapers when hearing his name. Remaining mail went into hidden alphabetical slots with a solid front, and a window containing a space below vertical bars for passing the mail. During these early "mail calls" in Mathews, any correspondence brought eager anticipation to the receiver.

1798 Subscription Paper recorded in *Records of Colonial Gloucester County, Virginia,* Volume 2, and page 81 by Polly Cary Mason reads:

"1798 Subscription Paper—For a Mail Carrier: We the subscribers wishing to employ [sic] ____back rider ... to ... from Mathews Court House to Gloucester Court House for one year next insueing after the fourteenth instant for the purpose of carrying and fetching letters and News Papers to the Subscribers to and from the Post Office in Gloucester. We do bind ourselves to Pay unto Mr. Richard Billups ... ...

Transportation of thirty five dollars in consideration of ... Said Richard Billups binds himself to furnish the above ... rider perform the tour ... regular the year round beginning the fourteenth instant, and that the said rider arrive at the Post Office in Gloster about the time the Northern mail arrives so as to receive Papers and Letters from the Mail and deliver those He carries so that they may be inclosed in the next, unavoidable accidents accepted. the Said Letters are to be delivered to the care of Mr. Henry Rispess at his Tavern at Mathews Court House. as witness our hands this ninth day of April Seventeen hundred and ....

"[Reverse side reads 'Lilly-Billups-Stoakes Family papers 'Contract for 1798'] Paid one dollar

John Atkinson (in part), William Fitchett, Armistead Smith, William Lane, Dudley Cary, Ch ^{R} Brown, Zadoc Litchfield, A^{brm} Van Bibber, _____ Hunley, Thomas Dawson, Henry Knight, Thomas Smith Junr, Joshua Brown, C. L. Briggs, Thomas Reynolds, James Van Bibber, Frances Armistead, Fran ^{cs} Whiting, H ^{dr} Hudgins, James H. Roy [scratched], J ^{as} Wilson, John Patterson."

Polly Cary Mason states in her book that the records she used were originals found in the attics of the Stoakes, Billups, Lillys and other homes. (Copied in pattern of the original handwritten copy)

POST OFFICE MAKES MANY MOVES

"Friendship is always a sweet responsibility, never an opportunity." Kahlil Gibran

During the Civil War and a bit afterward, Matthews Court House Post Office moved south to the site occupied today at the entrance to Riverside Convalescent Center. Joseph W. Owen took over the office In April 1870. During his term the post office moved back into the village and sat where Bay Cultural School operates today. It moved again with no record of a date to the corner of Main and Church Street, where the brick building, originally owned by Edgar and Wilbur Foster (Foster Brothers) sits. Their store served as a department store, and today Mathews Visitor's Center occupies one front corner of the first floor.

The records from the National Archives tell us that in April 1870, the spelling of Matthews had been corrected to "Mathews Court House Post Office." However they didn't change the name to "Mathews Post Office" until May 1893 when Grover Cleveland sat in the White House. It took place when Henry Sibley became postmaster, moving the post office to the family owned store, Sibley Brothers General Store. The business continued to operate under the Sibley name as a general merchandise store until November 2003, outliving all general merchandise stores of its type in the county though the post office continued moving. Most residents have heard Henry Sibley's motto:" If we don't have it at Sibley's, it isn't made." During my childhood, local folks told that in early days of toilet tissue being sold in this area, a customer asked for toilet paper. The late Henry Sibley innocently replied, "I don't have toilet paper, but I can give you some mighty fine sandpaper." Whether truth or a tale, the reader can make his decision, but my grandparents declared it true.

Griffith S. Marchant first became postmaster May 1897 and served until July 1914. During his tenancy, patrons grew in number with greater demands, and the United States Postal Service (USPS) demanded more from larger post offices. Therefore Mathews Post Office could no longer sit in the corner of a store but demanded its own building.

An article that the *Mathews Journal* published on October 2, 1913 states:" Work on the post-office is being rushed and it will be ready for occupancy sometime this week. Mr. Marchant declares that when complete the office will be the finest of its kind in this section of Virginia, being equipped with combination boxes and every convenience."

Wilber Shield accepted appointment in 1914, followed by Joseph E. Healy in 1916, while Marchant collected rent for the post office and conducted other business. He owned a dry goods store about this time, according to my mother, Grace R. Callis, who worked as a sales clerk a short time during Marchant's second stint as postmaster. He was appointed acting postmaster again October 1921, accepting the office of postmaster a second time in March 1922. He served until December 1933.

The political power in Washington D.C. determined who served in most post offices during those years. From the time Mathews Post Office moved into the new building referred to above, until today, the post office has had its own building although the location moved several times.

Sibley's General Store where Mathews Post Office sat in the corner 1893-1897 with Henry Sibley serving as postmaster. Photo taken in 2004, showing paved streets with sidewalks, electric wires and other more modern businesses unlike the early years the Sibley Brothers operated their general merchandise store.

"I'm certainly having the time of my life far away from confusion, turmoil and strife since it might be of interest. I will say at this juncture that we have mended our 23rd puncture." (1917 Post card face with picture of convertible with woman on back seat and young man, pushing a tire pump.)

Mathews Post Office Finds a Permanent Home

"Love in a letter endures forever in our memories."
Emily Post

When Marcellus B. Garnett became acting postmaster December 1933, he moved the post office to a building next to Hudgins Pharmacy. About 1940 Garnett moved the post office a second time when the brick building on Church Street, now owned by Dr. Robert J. Stewart, became available. The post office entrance of that day is now the site of a real estate office. The mail continued to arrive and leave the Church Street location after Garnett's retirement under Wallace Armistead, postmaster from 1948 until 1972.

During Armistead's term of service, the post office moved again. The late Herbert Gayle erected a building specifically for the Mathews Post Office, adjoining Gayle's Home Furnishings in 1958. The new building had updated lock boxes, requiring keys, for patrons instead of combination locks. Today the post office remains on that site, but the adjoining stores in the small strip mall have been demolished, making room for a Food Lion Store in the very back of the large lot.

June Rowe spent her working years from the early 1970's in Mathews Post Office, serving as postmaster until she retired April 1992. Others followed her, but today Dana Brown serves as postmaster, having seen Mathews Post office upgraded to class one in 2002.

Mathews Post Office sat at the end of the strip mall on Main Street, Mathews, Virginia, before the buildings beyond it were demolished in 2003, making room for a Food Lion back of the buildings with an enlarged parking lot. The post office section used in 2004 will be rebuilt.

The village, known still as Mathews Court House has changed. Actually, you reach the new county office buildings, banks and a shopping area before you leave Buckley Hall Road. Richardson's Drug Store has reopened its doors in late 2004, but offers no drugs. But the thing local folk and frequent visitors have missed since Mr. Richardson retired has returned—the soda fountain with breakfast and lunch specials.

Main Street has also changed: At the entrance, Hardee's welcomes one with fast food on the right—the unusual for Mathews Court House. Food Lion, with a Chinese carryout restaurant, has replaced the strip mall with its locally owned stores. Retail stores line the street except for the large library where "Farmers Bank of Mathews" operated for years. The building, now double its size, appeals to both adults and children. Bay Culture School of Arts, which offers retail and also classes, sits farther down the street in the store built by L.M. Callis for general merchandise and farm machinery.

Today on Church Street, where retail stores operated not too many years ago, a café and offices for doctors, lawyers, insurance companies, real estate brokers, investors and accountants occupy the buildings. On the corner of the Court Green, the Civil War Confederate soldier still greets everyone with his crossed hands. The old Court House stands stalwart with its unique arched second story window, dating it to the eighteenth century; the old clerk's office and jail make up the rest of the historical Court Green. Newer buildings sit on each end.

"If you don't enjoy what you have, how could you be happier with more?" Church Bulletin

North End and Belle Isle Post Offices Made Official

"Oft the pangs of absence are removed by a letter."
Old Valentine

On the route from Gloucester County, North End Post Office sat on Route 14, John Clayton Memorial Highway, near Route 617, North River Road. It was the forerunner of North Post Office and became official in 1808 with Jasper S. Clayton as postmaster. A total of 11 postmasters served before it was discontinued on August 22, 1866. The residents remained without a local post office for the next 18 years.

Records read: "On North River stood North End, the home of John Page, son of the Honorable Mann Page of Rosewell, and the great-grandson of Colonel John Page of Williamsburg, the immigrant. North End passed to the Van Bibber family and on October 21, 1821, Dr. Henry Wythe Tabb of Toddsbury married the only daughter of Andrew and Sarah Van Bibber." (Martin Diggs in *Mathews County Panorama* published by MCHS)

According to Dr. Tabb's diary, he lived at North End until he completed his new home, Auburn, in 1824. The manor sat on the point of land where the headwaters of the North River meet. We do not know whether the post office sat on the estate or near it.

Westward to Route 198, Buckley Hall Road, and south of North End Road to Route 694, Waverly Lane, in the vicinity of "Clifton," Belle Isle Post Office was established September 13, 1830 when Andrew Jackson served as President. It sat in a front corner of Thomas Lumpkin's general store, and he served as the only postmaster until it was discontinued January 1833. Other than the fact, Belle Isle General Merchandise Store was declared well stocked and prosperous in its day, nothing is recorded about Belle Isle.

Cobbs Creek Post Office Established

"Just one word of Consolation, sometimes sooths a breaking heart." Post Card 1912

Northwestward up Route 198, Buckley Hall Road, from Mathews Court House, the prominent Nicholas Cobb's family settled on a creek, flowing inland from near the head of the Piankatank River, in the mid 1600 period. Since Nicholas Cobb was the first white settler on the creek, it was known by his name—thus Cobbs Creek. Though the first survey shows the property located on Cobb's Creek, and the first published map, showing Cob Creek, appeared in 1683, but later issues showed the current spelling.

Settlers on the Piankitank in the area of Cobbs Creek grew in number. And in 1853 Alfred Billups wrote postal authorities the following: "Mr. Lawson says, and I believe it is the will of the petitioners that I must be appointed the postmaster at Cobbs Creek and I have certified as much below, and if your honorable chooses, I will accept it." (*Gloucester-Mathews Gazette-Journal* March 1, 1990)

Thus in December 1853, Cobb's Creek Post Office became official, but the name wasn't changed to Cobbs Creek until 1894. Like most other post offices it sat in the front corner of a general-merchandise store. I've located nothing to tell me whether Mr. Lumpton owned and operated the store where the office would sit in 1853. However it seems probable.

We have records of several postmasters after Billups, but the only other statistic from the National Archives shows the post office had been discontinued from November 17, 1856 until March 23, 1857. Benjamin Blake served both before and after this interruption in the mail delivery, but I find no explanation for it.

In 1934, the post office moved from Emmett W. Matthews' store south on Route 198, Buckley Hall Road, to William F. Williams' store when his wife, Vernah Collie Williams, became postmaster. Besides general merchandise, barber and millinery shops were also located within its walls. Before the post office moved into Williams' store, he operated a lunchroom, with fountain service and a marble counter in the store. The service catered to students of Cobbs Creek High School, which sat across the road. Vernah changed that setup, removing the lunchroom, when the post office moved into the same corner of the store. She retired in 1960 after 26 years of service.

When Vernah Williams retired, Vernah and William Williams' daughter, Anne Williams Diggs, became the new postmaster. During Diggs service as postmaster, the post office began to outgrow its quarters with an influx of new residents yet it was seven years after she retired before it moved across the road to the building that had housed Cobbs Creek School, now a part of the Industrial Park.

On October 8-14, 1983 Anne Diggs attended the 79th annual convention of the National Association of Postmasters of the United States, held in San Juan, Puerto Rico. During the convention, she received one of the five "Postmaster of the Year" awards for her excellent service. One honoree was selected from each Direct Mail Marketing Association. The awards had been based on criteria such as portrayal of the Postal Service image and service to customers.

Diggs retired in 1982 after 24 years, serving the one post. Three years later in January 1985, her daughter and Vernah Williams' granddaughter, Colanne Diggs Bunting, accepted the position. She remains postmaster today, reporting 520 rented post office boxes with more available and 160 Star Route customers.

Cobbs Creek community worshipped at Mathews Chapel United Methodist Church or Spring Hill Baptist Church, and the blacks attended Ebenezer Baptist Church. I find no record of their private schools though they had them in every community--unless the one-room "primer" down Cobbs Lane came under that category. After about 1910, white children attended Cobbs Creek School that taught grades one through high school in the its early years. Mrs. Fitchett, who taught at Cobbs Creek School, believed it to be the first accredited high school in the county. In 1939, Cobbs Creek High School became a grammar school with the older students, joining the rest of the county in the new consolidated high school. In later years, the school closed when schools integrated, moving all the county's schoolchildren to Lee Jackson Grammar School, Thomas

Hunter Middle School and Mathews High School. The school had also served as a social center for the students, their parents and grandparents through the years. Today, the brick edifice next to the industrial park houses the post office and other businesses. At a recent 60th year class reunion for Mathews High School class of 1944, I was a guest, representing my husband—a part of the class. I heard former classmates talking about experiences and fun they had in their years at Cobbs Creek School.

In the 1980s, Edith Lane Burrell and Marcello Williams gave a *Gloucester-Mathews Gazette-Journal* reporter information, concerning the black community in the late 1800s and into the twentieth century. Burrell's father, Musco Lane, had a general merchandise store at the intersection of Route 198, Buckley Hall Road and Route 630, Roane Point Drive. Lane not only operated a store, but also a tomato-canning factory, a crab-picking house, a movie theater near his store and fairgrounds at Grubbs bottom (a lowland between Blakes and Hudgins). Burrell explained that fairs weren't segregated like schools, churches and even stores because folks had little entertainment in those days so everyone came to a fair.

Lane had the good fortune of some education. His mother had been born into slavery on the home place of Captain Frank Haynes, who lived on Route 629, Ebenezer Church Road. Captain and Mrs. Haynes had chosen her to work in the home. She kept the position of housekeeper after she received her freedom and married. When her son was born in the 1880s, there were few if any schools for Negroes, according to Mrs. Burrell--an African-American. Mrs. Haynes determined that the boy should learn to read and write so she taught him herself.

In an interview with Marcella Williams, she related that her mother had attended the first school for blacks in the area. The building sat in front of Ebenezer Church. Miss Williams herself attended what the reporter felt had been a crowded school. This one-room school sat a bit east of the first on Buckley Hall Road, teaching children from Cobbs Creek, Hallieford and Blakes. In 1919, the school moved to Blakes, occupying the Old Samaritan Hall. It had two stories with the lower grades on the first floor and the higher grades upstairs. They used that school until monies from the Rosenwald fund, which was established early in the twentieth century solely for the construction of schools for black students, assisted the county to build a three-room school in the 1920s.

Mathews County officials only financed the school to operate five months. Parents paid for two months, but they were short two months offered the white children. The county discontinued the school after building Thomas Hunter School that offered nine months schooling for the black children.

Courtesy the *Gloucester-Mathews Gazette-Journal*

Cobbs Creek Post Office 1983 in Williams' store with retired postmaster Anne Williams Diggs at the door

Social Life in the Rural Communities

"The word, even the most contradictory word, preserves contact—it is silence which isolates." Thomas Mann

One might wonder what people did for pleasure in Mathews County during the nineteenth century. My research shows the residents did the same things basically as they did most of the first quarter of the twentieth century in rural areas on the east coast of the mid Atlantic.

The isolated general merchandise store, where a post office sat in the corner, became the center of each community with little contrast between them. The business not only furnished groceries, dry goods, kitchen utensils, farm supplies and catalogs to order furniture, including smaller household items, but social life for the residents. Their other contact with each other was at Sunday worship services, but this split the communities into groups— Methodists, Baptists, Episcopalians and a few Quakers— both Quiet and Evangelical.

If any of the women, whose home obligations permitted them to visit the store alone, it was during the day. They walked, drove the horse and buggy or in later years a car, to the nearby store to post and fetch mail, shop and visit. Before and during World War II, most families' purchased groceries not grown on the farm with eggs, chickens or butter. If the bartering storekeeper owed them money, he gave a due bill, or if they owed him, he charged the difference. Some of the larger stores gave round tokens with the business name and designated amounts printed on them, instead of the slip of paper the smaller stores used. There were only a few cash customers in the early years.

When women had their day out, they not only shopped, but also posted any letters and fetched the family's mail. If several gathered after lunch on Wednesdays or

Thursdays, they enjoyed a chat with their neighbors, gathering the latest news—births, engagements, marriages, any illness and deaths. And sometimes a bit of gossip slipped into the conversation with whispers. Some visited in the store, but the porch was a favorite gathering spot in warm weather. They only bought what they could carry easily if walking.

In the late 1930s and 1940s, Momma taught me to wash on Monday, iron on Tuesday, catch up or have some time for myself on Wednesday, sew or do special cooking on Thursdays, clean the entire ten-room house on Friday and cook on Saturdays. Sunday was Sunday School and church service, followed by a scrumptious meal that had for the most part been prepared on Saturday. Then each did what suited them. Sometimes we all piled in the automobile and visited relatives too far away to have time to visit on a weekday. In my teen years, my folks usually rested while we young people enjoyed relaxing walks, reading or when friends had joined us, we often just chatted. If it rained on Monday, we still washed, hanging the clothes on the enclosed porches. Earlier, Momma hung the clothes in unused rooms that hadn't been refurbished and on a side porch with heavy-cotton twine lines. During canning season, we got little sewing or extras done on Wednesdays and Thursdays, but picked, prepared and canned—vegetables and fruits. Daddy gathered the tomatoes and corn that he felt too much for Momma and us girls before he went in the fields or out delivering farm products to stores in the county. Of course, he didn't do the latter until after 1940 when he had an automobile to use.

In the years through the 1950s and for the most part much later, businesses other than those who sold prepared food closed on Sunday. The Mathews Hotel, Pine Hall, Davis and South Hotels and those I don't recall stayed open in their day seven days a week. They closed at different intervals, depending on circumstances—fire and death or just too old to do the work required.

Merchants welcomed wagons with crates of chickens that they could ship on the next steamboat and later by truck to nearby cities. Some of the robust women caught and delivered the fowl, but I never knew any in my day. Daddy would say, "That's a man-sized job."

Most of the men in the community gathered in the general-merchandise store nightly except on Sundays. They stayed inside, sitting around the store on nail kegs and later stools were added. By the 1940s folding chairs appeared according to pictures of the era. Dorothy Diggs White, who lives near the old Blakes Post office, said her daddy, Emmett went to Diggs Post Office and store evenings as a teenager. His father, Bailey Diggs, let Emmett accompany him when he was younger than most boys, due to the fact his mother had died. Emmett's half siblings by Bailey's second wife were only tots. So Emmett felt himself a loner. If the seats gave out, some men ambled back to the plump bags of feed to sit. In cold weather, the tin-wood-burning stove (a few stores had pot-belly stoves) drew the patrons inside. But in summer, the porch proved popular when the store became crowded. In every store, they caught up on the news whether national, state, local or just what was happening in the neighborhood. On rainy or snowy days, a few men found a keg or stool near the store's pot bellied stove. It served as a place to pass the time of day, retreating from crying babies or nagging wives. Though most only stayed long enough to get warm before the trek back home.

Some storekeepers furnished checkerboards for those interested, and a spittoon or a bucket with a bit of sand was essential to accommodate those who chewed tobacco, requiring them to spit tobacco juice often. Emmett Diggs' daughter, Dorothy Diggs White, said that her dad told his children about the big copper spittoon at Diggs, most likely in Jessie Hudgins' store or one nearer his home where Ocean Products now operates. If anyone played their harmonica, guitar or fiddle, they might be encouraged to bring it certain evenings. It added to the enjoyment with feet tapping to the music. Many of the men smoked their pipes, cigars and later cigarettes, causing every man to go home with the smells imbedded in their clothing.

Politicians knew where to find the county's men when campaigning. The candidates visited different stores in their precinct, or in the county if the election included a county official, each night, rotating from one to another, near election time.

"Gilmour Diggs from Beaverlette said men stayed in his great grandfather's store until midnight playing cards and exchanging news. 'Rook' was the favorite card game. They made sandwiches, buying the ingredients from the storekeeper and had a good time.

"Brooke Ripley said she stayed up and waited for her husband to get the day's news occurring in the community. Only men frequented the place at night."(*Mathews-Gloucester Gazette Journal* November 7, 1982)

If the community needed to raise money for a project, the housewives provided homemade ice cream and both pound and layer cakes, or pies, fresh from the oven, to sell by the dish or slice. Before plastic spoons and forks or paper plates existed, someone or all provided dishes and silverware. These socials were held early in the evening and were considered great times especially if someone provided music. In some communities, pie and ice cream socials were held in community halls of one type or another.

Growth Required More Post Offices

"Love in a letter endures forever in our memories."
Emily Post

One may wonder how the county grew. Most plantation owners had large families; and when a son married, the father gave him a plot of land, helping him build his house. A plot sufficient for a family in the nineteenth century was 10 or more acres according to information *The 1850 Federal Census* gives. We find records of daughters marrying local men, but many married men from other counties, states or recent arrivals from European countries. Generally if the couple, with the husband from elsewhere, made their residence in Mathews County, they lived with her parents for a time. If the husband had obtained land, they built or moved into the house he had already erected. Some constructed their homes on a plot on the wife's father's property. More families made need for more post offices in the front corner of the general merchandise stores.

Hicks Wharf Has First Post Office on East River

"Make not my ear a stranger be to your thoughts."
Joseph Addison

On the western shores of East River, Hicks Wharf received shipments by steamboats. The store and wharf sat off East River Road at the end Route 650—now Hicks Wharf Road. The large pier, where the schooners and later steamers landed before 1933, no longer exists. I learned in 1979 that one might travel near shore in a skiff and find remains of pilings that held the wharf in place before the great Atlantic Hurricane of August 1933. However the two-story home still sat to the right and remains under new ownership today. The Davis family occupied the house in the nineteenth and most of the twentieth centuries. In the sunshine on the day I chatted with Inez Davis, daughter of William and Annie, the white paint and green shutters glistened so brightly, one wouldn't know the structure was that old except for the style of the architecture.

Though the post office bore his name, William E. Hicks didn't become postmaster until nine years after Hicks Wharf Post Office had been recorded in October 1869 with Samuel Clarke as postmaster. How much politics influenced his appointment is anyone's guess. Like all post offices in the early days, it sat in the front corner of a general store.

Charles Treakle rowed from the opposite side of East River, both morning and evening, the years that he served as postmaster. Wonder how many stormy days the river prevented the trip, and the storekeeper had to take care of the mail? Or did Treakle ever have to spend the night with someone at Hicks Wharf while his family worried about his safety?

Both William A. Davis and his wife, Annie, served as postmasters until Susanne S. Hicks took the position in 1930. She remained in office until October 1933 when the Post Office Department closed Hicks Wharf Post Office, sending the mail to Miles. The August Hurricane of that year shifted mail arriving in the county by steamboats, which had few places to dock, to total dependency on land delivery.

Whoever wrote the postman's motto wisely included "Through rain and storm and gloom at night..." because the history of brave men and women who served their fellow citizens behind iron bars of the Post Office's teller windows experienced plenty of every kind of inclement weather. One memorable storm in August 1933 washed over Mathews, Virginia, with such force it knocked out Hicks Wharf and the warehouse and gave new meaning to "Gloom of night...."

Television didn't exist, forewarning residents of the coming storm. Few had radios and fewer had telephones; and since the storm originated in the waters off the Carolinas, Virginia residents had no warning ahead of time to batter down their homes and businesses.

The howling gale raged first from northeast, pushing the waters outlining Mathews County, higher and higher. After the eye passed, bringing stillness, the winds shifted southeast and continued its velocity, lashing the waters into the high seas. Such force of water with high winds played havoc with everything in its path, swishing objects to and fro.

In the casual conversation I had with Inez Davis in 1979 revealed how much life at the wharf had changed. She said that she still enjoyed the view of her sweeping lawn, tapering down to the water and traffic on the large river. We could see sail and motorboats, moving up and down East River as we talked. But Davis still missed the active times when the wharf, which once stood to our left, had been busy as a city street on weekdays. She had been a teen-ager when the storm hit.

Port Haywood Post Office

"The post-office had a great charm at one period in our lives." Jane Austen

By 1870 the 200 families, who lived four miles south of Mathews Court House, made up a sizable community. They had become tired of the infrequent trips to Mathews Court House, fetching the mail. So they demanded a post office in the front corner of Charles Hudgins General Store that sat on route 14, New Point Comfort Highway. After all, the general store had everything else they needed to purchase.

Shortly before the application was filed, the men, who gathered in the store nights, assisted in the search for a suitable name. Then one reminded them of a stormy evening, when a soaked weather-beaten waterman had limped into the store, having walked from East River. The man introduced himself as Captain Haywood, saying the rough seas had forced him to take refuge in a protected harbor at an inlet off East River. After securing the boat, Haywood walked eastward down the sandy road until he reached an intersection with a general store.

He declared the place was "Port Haywood," a good port for any waterman during a storm, but it took a Haywood to discover the place. Years later Mrs. Ladie B. Hudgins, who served as acting postmistress and clerk of Port Haywood Post Office from July 16, 1923 until July 11, 1973, told a reporter, "I bet he was from Guinea." (Guinea, a part of Gloucester County, has many residents named Haywood and also many watermen.)

The men, making up the community, and the applicant felt Port Haywood an appropriate name for the post office. The officials must have agreed since it became official on April 13, 1871 with Charles H. Hudgins serving as postmaster.

Records from the *Gloucester-Mathews Gazette-Journal* archives tell that the new stately building stands in the same spot as the original post office. Documentation from the Washington D.C. Archives proves that Port Haywood Post Office was discontinued on October 31, 1921, when the mail had been sent to Traders Post Office. Then the post office was re-established January 14, 1922 with George C. Hunt as postmaster. Over a year later in July 1923, Ladie A. Brownley, whom most people know as "Miss Ladie," became acting postmistress. At that time, the post office sat in the old Dr. Littleberry (known as Berry) Foster Office building across the road from the original and present post office.

During her first days of service at age 19, Ladie walked four miles to the work she enjoyed. Not only did she tend the mail, but she also enjoyed her most frequent visitor, William Irving Hudgins. And she knew Hudgins would take her home in his new Model T at the close of the day.

"Miss Ladie" related that only three families received Christmas cards her first year in the post office. The mail arrived by truck in later years, but before that, it came by boat to Williams Wharf, having to be hauled to Port

Haywood. In those days postcards went for one cent and letters for two cents.

Hudgins is quoted in the July19, 1973 issue of the *Gloucester-Mathews Gazette-Journal* saying, "I used to go to the post office and take her home. When President Harding died, they closed the post office down and we went riding in the rain in my $408 Model T Ford." The same year "Miss Ladie" received the Model T as an engagement gift.

Shortly after "Miss Ladie" and Hudgins were married in 1924, he became postmaster, and "Miss Ladie" served as clerk of Port Haywood—just a new name for the job she had been doing well.

Mr. and Mrs. Hudgins lived in the two-story house with a green lawn back of the store and post office. They also raised their two daughters, Mrs. Virginia Dare Sadler and Mrs. Rosalyn White, at Port Haywood.

Mrs. Hudgins said to the *Gloucester-Mathews Gazette-Journal* reporter, "We spent many happy hours at Port Haywood." The post office stayed open from 6:30 a.m. to 10 p.m. each weekday, and they accumulated many memories in their store from the first day. Mr. Hudgins got to work in the store and post office early mornings, and he cared for both evenings when "Miss Ladie" did household chores, giving time to raising their daughters.

In 1950, Mr. Hudgins built a new smaller building for the post office, moving it from the store to the new building. Mail went by Highway Carrier to Star Route patrons, desiring the service, and locked boxes served others. But when all boxes had been rented, new residents placed their names on a waiting list, receiving their mail by general delivery until a box became available. These services created more efficient service. Today, that building houses a nail care business.

Port Haywood upgraded from a fourth class office to third class on July 1, 1955. Mr. Hudgins retired as postmaster December 31, 1963, and Gertrude Hurst replaced him in the position. But "Miss Ladie" remained as clerk ten more years.

Ladie Hudgins, who was 69 years old, retired from her position Wednesday, July 11, 1973. The *Gloucester-Mathews Gazette-Journal* quoted Mrs. Hudgins in the abovementioned article, "I have grown to love the post office." As a retirement gift for her fifty years of service in the post office, her husband purchased the Dr. Foster building, moving it across the road to his property with only one mishap. The telephone lines caught on the chimney, causing it to tumble onto the roof--a repairable mishap. "I don't know exactly what I'm going to do with it, but it's where we did our courting," Mr. Hudgins said.

Port Haywood Post Office sat in Dr. Littleberry Foster's building when "Miss Ladie" began working as the assistant postmaster in 1923. Today the building has been improved in appearance with shutters and awning. The new post office sits back from the road in the background of the picture.

"Miss Ladie" made many friends and few if any enemies during her years of service in Port Haywood Post Office. Even years later when she sat at home in a wheel chair, rolling about the kitchen preparing tasty dishes to serve her family, I found that she had a smile and kind word for her visitors.

She served under Postmaster Gertrude Hurst, who performed from July 5, 1963 until 1989. The post office had outgrown the building that had been efficient in 1950. During the year that Hurst retired, the post office moved into the new larger brick building with post office boxes available to everyone except those on the Star Route.

For some months after Hurst retired, Officers in Charge kept the post office operating. But in January 7, 1990, Robert Mallory, who left a division of the postal service in Richmond, Virginia, and moved into the community, filled the position. When Mallory retired in July 1999, Roberta Ringstaff became postmaster. She serves today with 308 post office boxes rented and 200 Star Route customers.

"We have no general delivery today," Ringstaff said in an interview.

Social Life from Another's View

When out searching for pictures of closed post offices, my daughter, Susan Adams, and I traveled to the apartment of Virginia Downs Adams in West Point, Virginia. She told that in the 1930s her daddy, Charlie Downs, would load his family in the car with a bucket of eggs and travel to Port Haywood to load up on groceries. After he and his wife, Hattie, made their purchases, Charlie joined the men on one side of the store and Hattie would join the women on the other side. She played with the other children, remembering Rosalyn Hudgins (now a White) best.

It was the family's evening out. If she remembered how late they stayed she failed to mention it.

Cricket Hill Post Office Sat on Milford Haven

"Never give up, for that is just the place and time that the tide will turn." Harriet Beecher Stowe

Cricket Hill became the seventh post office in Mathews County. I turn left on Mill Point Drive off Route 223, Cricket Hill Road, just before the U.S. Coast Guard Station and go to the end. The store with a post office sat on the right side of the drive. I wonder why the name Cricket Hill? Pouring through reference books, I'm not quite satisfied until I confer with a lifetime resident, Judy Ward, who wrote and directed a reenactment of the *Battle of Cricket Hill* from her research in 1976.

During the Revolutionary War, Lord Dunmore, the last colonial governor in Virginia, left Hampton Roads after the burning of Norfolk with his whole fleet. They landed on Gwynn's Island June 1, 1776. Dunmore fortified himself and entrenched the island with about 500 men.

Meanwhile, General Andrew Lewis commanded the Continental Army, who camped to the south, across the waters of Milford Haven. Lewis threw up fortifications and mounted his great guns behind the hill, which surrounded the shoreline. In an interview with Judy Ward, I learned when Lord Dunmore saw the Continental troops coming over the hill, he said in jest that they looked like crickets. Since that day, the location has been known as "Cricket Hill."

Though Lord Dunmore made light of the American Revolutionists, he suffered a staggering defeat at their hands. Dunmore retreated on July 9, 1776, having undergone heavy losses of men and his fleet suffered some thousand pounds worth of damage. (*History and Progress, Mathews County, Virginia*, provided many facts that Judy confirmed.)

The *Virginian Gazette* reported, referring to the Continental Army: "In this affair, we lost not a man but poor Captain Arundel, who was killed by the bursting of a mortar of his own invention, although the general and all the officers were against his firing it."

The view from the hills, overlooking Milford Haven, drew settlers to build waterfront homes. After Belle Isle Post Office closed in 1833, these homeowners had to travel miles to Mathews Court House, securing their mail, perhaps once a week.

In 1873, William N. Trader, who not only owned a plantation on Milford Haven, but also dallied in many business endeavors, felt it time the community had its own post office. Though mail came and left, the cancellation read Mathews, Virginia. The United States Post Office Department didn't officially record Cricket Hill Post Office, issuing their cancellation stamp, until February 2, 1874. Trader served as the first postmaster. Like the other post offices, it sat in the corner of a general store and the public dealt with an assistant.

Cricket Hill boasted a busy business community in the late nineteenth and early twentieth centuries. The first decade the post office officially operated, it not only served local families but also the citizens across Milford Haven on Gwynn's Island, who sculled a canoe or skiff across the waters to pick up their mail.

In the early twentieth century, the Baltimore Steamer, which traveled up the Piankitank River as far as Freeport in Gloucester County, made Cricket Hill one of its ports of entry. Wherever a steamboat docked, business boomed because the citizens found it the best source to ship seafood, lumber, fowl and other local products. In turn the steamboat brought commodities to the folk living in the area. They delivered mail from the North for the area, merchandise for the local store and items that local residents ordered from Baltimore.

Seven postmasters served before the post office closed with William F. Marchant serving the longest. He began service in September 1897 and served until October 1923, having closed the office for a short period in 1919. Charles N. Majette followed Marchant as postmaster. After the August 1933 Storm, Cricket Hill Post Office closed for a short period a second time to rebuild. Leslie Horsley became postmaster in December 1937 and served until the post office closed. I contacted Mary Majette Jarvis in early 2004, regarding her memory of the post office. She said, "It was in my granddaddy's store."

After the Baltimore Steamer ceased its run to Cricket Hill in August 1933, and a modern bridge replaced the ferry in 1939, Cricket Hill's business vanished. The post office closed September 1941, and the mail was routed to Redart Post Office.

Mathews Court House still in operation as it has been well over 200 years. Paint has been redone and sidewalks, lighting fixtures and grass have been added to the bare area of the nineteenth century. The building will be used for special events when the Court House moves to larger quarters on Buckley Hall Road.

Chapter Two

Mail Arrives by Steamboats and Trucks

Traders Post Office

"The post-office appeared a singularly domestic institution here. Ever and anon the stage stopped before some low shop or dwelling." Henry David Thoreau

The East River site south of Mathews Court House at the end of Route 606, Diggs Wharf Road, had been known originally as Cronies Bluff. However, after Andrew J. Diggs built a wharf with a warehouse and general merchandise store, the name changed to "Diggs Wharf." Since the Old Dominion Steamship Company's steamboats visited the wharf daily, business boomed for some years. By early 1878, they realized the need for a post office.

William N. Trader became the first postmaster in March 1878, the post office bearing his name. This date overlaps the years Trader served as postmaster of Cricket Hill. However, Trader didn't actually work in the post offices but depended on assistants. As postmaster, Trader became responsible for tallying receipts, mailing the records and monies regularly. Wonder who made the most money? Was it the postmaster or the one who worked long hours?

The post office operated in a separate building from the general merchandise store in its early years. But when Andrew J. Diggs became postmaster 21 years later in December 1899, the post office sat in one corner of his store. In an interview with Diggs' granddaughter, Jane Diggs Curfman, she knew he sold his store to Ollie R. Gayle, 12 years later in December 1911. His wife Gladys Gayle became postmaster at the time, serving to May 1917.

While Gayle served as postmaster, Bertha Hudgins was her assistant, according to Bertha's daughter Gladys Hammond, former treasurer of Mathews County, in a 2003 interview. Baby Gladys entered the world in May 1914. When Bertha became strong enough to work, she took Gladys to work every day. Carrying the baby in a basket, she sat it under the counter and went about her duties. She tended Gladys only when necessary during the busy hours when she cancelled outgoing mail before the mail truck arrived. Then it became her duty to sort the incoming letters, newspapers and magazines and place each bundle in the family's pigeonhole on the inside of the wood and iron cage. Bertha stored any parcel post packages under the counter beyond the baby's basket, placing a notation regarding packages in the box with their mail. If a member of any family was in the building when she completed the individual organization and called the family names, she handed their mail over the counter. But I believe that later in the day when customers came to just gather their mail, she delighted in showing off her baby girl, whom she cuddled. Yet, imagine what today's Postal Inspector would say when he heard a hidden baby wail upon entering the post office.

Oscar L. Jagger became postmaster in 1917, relieving Bertha Hudgins of her duties. He served little over four years. But when Mammie Powell received an official appointment in 1921, she declined the offer, preferring to serve as an assistant. Guess she didn't want responsibility. Omega L. Powell accepted the position in May 1922 and served until the post office was discontinued September 1923, sending the mail to Port Haywood.

Floyd Hurst also operated a store near Traders Post Office, which burnt in April 1908 with a total loss of $4,500—a good sum in that day. But I could find no record of the type merchandise he carried. (Information from *Mathews Journal*)

Since the post office closed, Trader is practically forgotten with people referring to the area as Diggs Wharf. But today even the wharf has disappeared. There are homes and lawns with any other acreage used for pastureland and hay crops.

What a coincidence, the wharf consumed Traders. In return, landscaping around new homes with their own piers swallowed the old wharf.

Williams Wharf Post Office

"The best love-letters are the direct promptings of the heart." Carleton C. Case

Mathews County natives can be found across the United States, especially in Virginia's large cities. My great uncle from the Glebe just southwest of Mathews Post Office, later Retz Post Office, founded W. Fred Richardson Security Storage Company, Richmond, Virginia. He edited and published booklets to send his customers monthly in 1927. I find quotations and his writings rich in character.

"Tomorrow will be the result of today's happiness."
The Richardson Review September 1927

North of Diggs Wharf, Williams Wharf was the largest port of call on East River. Eighteenth and nineteenth century homes sit up lanes or on the highway near the wharf area. The early colonists built a chapel for worship once they settled. The first was known as "Kingstone." It fell, as did some afterwards, due to fire or neglect. When the chapel built about 1840 burnt, the late Milton Murray salvaged the handmade-colonial bricks from the ruins to help build the slightly larger edifice. So Christ Church, which was built in the 1903, stands erect and in good repair today.

Pulling away from the churchyard and heading towards the wharf, a historical marker appears, standing in front of a house. It reads:" The Customs House." The stately building, which housed a store and the post office, has been converted into a home. But I learn from Betty Ann Murray Richardson that the owners have records from the "Custom House," a smaller building that no longer exists.

Fifty-one-year-old Samuel Williams left Eastern Shore, moving to Mathews about 1776. He brought his third wife, having buried his first two, and 10 of his 11 children. Williams purchased several plats of land, totaling 725 acres and including two colonial houses, a store, a warehouse, a water mill and a building to house the Custom House were included in the purchase. About 1782 either Samuel Williams or his son Thomas built the main house on the Estate, "Poplar Grove," known at that time as "East Warehouse." Today, Poplar Grove has its own road off New Point Comfort Highway. However, the modern highway and roads do not tell us how many roads ran from plantation to plantation or whether the present highway existed. The house at Poplar Grove only consisted of today's West Wing backing its early days. The warehouse, though a dwelling, also housed luxuries from abroad until the owner picked up the merchandise. Boats, known as "lighters" unloaded ships since there was no wharf until about 1830. The goods was brought ashore and distributed to the buyer or stored in various locations used as warehouses until called for. (Information from *History and Progress of Mathews County, Virginia*" published by MCHS)

The general store kept a varied assortment of items: Sugar, salt, flour, molasses, whisky, farming tools, nails, clothing and all sorts of other dry goods. Barrels of fish, and doubtless oysters and clams, sat ready for customers, who came a distance to pick up their freight and cart it home. They could buy the barrel or broken quantities.

"Mathews was the official port of entry for the registration of all U.S. and foreign vessels from 1802 to

35

1844. During this period the U.S. archives show that over 10,000 vessels called at the "East River" port. The Custom House, located at Williams Wharf, was the center for maritime activities in Mathews County. It was there the owners, merchants, riggers, chandlers, etc. met to do business. By 1808 a carriage service operated from Williams Wharf to Mathews Court House. A 1780 tax record shows that Samuel Williams paid 213 pounds sterling in taxes—a huge amount for that day but verifies the huge volume of traffic through the port of Williams Wharf."(John W. Bateman in *Gloucester-Mathews Gazette Journal*).

Samuel Williams' grandson, William Williams, built the wharf, using ballast bricks, which were accumulated over the years off ships that left them, for the foundation of the wharf. Once the wharf sat completed, ships from England brought ballast and cargo, leaving with all types of products that Mathews County residents produced. There were hundreds of pounds of tobacco, cattle, horses, hogs, and other non-perishable items shipped. Other ships carried barrels of crabs, oysters, clams and grain.

Though no post office existed, mail had been coming by boat to the local residents during those prosperous years of the late eighteenth and early nineteenth centuries. The seas served as the most convenient highways in the coastal areas for mail delivery. And documentation proves Williams Wharf participated in these deliveries.

"Excerpts from an account book of William Williams, customs and wharf agent at Williams Wharf during the middle years of the nineteenth century.

"Steamer Coffee and Owners, September 30, 1855.

To: William Williams, debtor

To 3 months from the first of July to the 30th of September 1855 inclusive carrying the U.S. Mail twice a week on Tuesdays and Saturdays from my wharf to Mathews Court House and back to my wharf at $75,00 per annum. One quarter, $18.75."

*****

"Williams Wharf,

Mathews County, Virginia

Steamer Coffee and Owners, 1856

To: William Williams:

> To wharfage and carrying U. S. Mail twice a week from Mathews Court House and back to my wharf from the first of January to the thirty first of Mar, 1856, inclusive, one quarter at $200.00 per annum, $50.00.

> Received the above $50.00 in full.

> William Williams"

(Copied exactly as originally written. From *History and Progress, Mathews County, Virginia,"* published by Mathews County Historical Society.)

Williams Wharf Post Office and store serves as a stately home today.

In December 1878, Benjamin Williams wrote, requesting a U.S. Post Office at Williams Wharf, named "Kingston." The Post Office Officials granted the post office but named it "Williams Wharf Post Office." Benjamin Williams served as postmaster from January 1879 until February 1896.

During the early to mid nineteenth century, some of Samuel William's descendents drifted to Baltimore, making that city their home. Cordelier, who lived in the city, married a Mr. Murray, some 35 years her senior. He purchased a summer home in Mathews where she could bring their children to vacation in the summers. A son, William H. C. Murray, either fell in love with the county or a local girl, making the county his residence. He married Elsie Williams, another descendent of Samuel Williams, of Susan Post Office. Murray was appointed Postmaster at Williams Wharf in February 1896 and served for 22 years. The post office remained in the family store with postmasters being all family members during its duration, closing in June 1943.

The Hurricane of 1933 changed business and post office deliveries throughout the entire county, and by then most local residents had access to an automobile to travel the few miles to town—Mathews Court House. Williams Wharf, like Hicks Wharf, was destroyed in the high winds and tidal wave on the fateful August morning. Thus after that date, deliveries came by trucks instead of steamboats. Mail for Williams Wharf went to Mathews Post Office after the 1943 closing. The Federal style store building was converted into stately home after that date.

New Point Post Office Established

"I know of me you often think.
But won't you do it please in ink?"
Anonymous

Travel south on Route 14, New Point Comfort Highway, to Sandbank Road where one will find New Point Post Office. Continuing eastward after turning onto Sandbank Road, I know the Chesapeake Bay must be a bit choppy because sea gulls have left the waters and fill the fields, feasting on any grain left at harvest. The view intensifies near the post office and store. This is the first post office to have taken us almost to the Bay--away from the rivers and havens.

Settlers, who first ventured into this southern end of the peninsula known as Mathews County, found fertile soil when they cleared a space and began cultivation. However, a richer find was the abundance of seafood, which the Chesapeake Bay on the east and Mobjack Bay on the west furnished. Word spread and one by one, young couples began with a small house on a plot of land off Grandpa's or even Great-Grandpa's grant. After the Civil War ended, the survivors settled with their families to rebuild and make a living. They didn't often have time to travel back to Port Haywood to post and fetch their mail. So in 1879 they applied for a post office. The Post Office Department appointed William F. Jarvis the first postmaster in June 1879.

There is no question as to how the name had been selected since it sat near the vicinity of New Point Lighthouse on New Point Comfort. It was April 1804 when Elzy Burroughs had conveyed two acres of land on New Point Comfort to the United States for $150. In October of the same year, the Governor of Virginia ceded "all the jurisdiction which this Commonwealth possesses over the said two acres of land were conveyed to the said United States by the before referred to indenture from Elzy Burroughs to the said United States provided a light house was erected within seven years, kept in repair and supported at the expense of the United States on same ...". The lighthouse had been completed and in use before 1810 with larger appropriations from the United States government granted over several years. The light guided ship captains into both the Mobjack and Chesapeake Bays, and reports were made as early as 1853 that the Bay Light also served the York River. (Information and quotation from *History and Progress Mathews County, Virginia* by Mathews County Historical Society)

Jarvis, who also had a small store on the right side of Sandbank Road, served as postmaster for ten years. John B. Grinnell, though just an older teenager, served one month; and E.H. Grinnell for almost three months before Isaac M. Hudgins became postmaster in October 1889. The post office moved across the road to Irving Preston Hudgins' store, later known as I.P. Hudgins & Son, in the second decade of the twentieth century. The Hudgins, all relatives, were postmasters until October 1986 through five generations.

Hubert Hudgins retired October 1986, ending almost a century of a member of his family managing New Point Post Office. He had begun his work in the post office in 1933 when New Point had fewer patrons than the 120, he reported upon retirement. Hubert enjoyed telling how his grandfather, William O. Hudgins put aside a waterman's life to become postmaster in 1897, serving until 1914.

Hubert enjoyed his life, owning and managing a general merchandise store and serving as postmaster. He informed a *Gloucester-Mathews Gazette-Journal* reporter that through the years he had worked "every day except Sundays and two separate weeks he was ill."

Hubert's sister, Mrs. William C. Burroughs, who lived near the store and post office, assisted him on Saturdays and when he needed to be out of the building. But Hubert credited his wife, Mae, for his longevity and success in the post office. "She's been all the help to me," he stated. "She's the one who helped me with all the forms and quarterly reports I had to keep."

It was Mae Hudgins who encouraged Hubert to retire. "She thinks it's time I start slowing down," he told the reporter. "But I'll still be running the store. I've got a whole lots of years to go there yet." And he did just that, but they died within months of each other in the late 1990s. (Quotations from the *Gloucester-Mathews Gazette-Journal*)

Helen Hurst followed the Hudgins family in New Point Post Office. She worked as OIC until Elizabeth Rowe became postmaster in December 1987. Rowe manned the office until early in 2001. In 1989 during her interim, Hubert Hudgins, who still owned and operated the store, built a cement block addition to the frame building, to house the post office. By doing so, patrons' rental boxes could be accessed day or night, meeting Federal requirements.

An OIC kept New Point Post Office operating after Rowe's retirement until December 3, 2001, when Cathy Vrablitz became postmaster. Perhaps Vrablitz will claim the position as long as Rowe did. She reports 123 rented post office boxes and nine Star Route highway deliveries in 2004.

New Point Post Office sat in the corner of the store owned by I. P. Hudgins & Son most of a century before it moved to an adjoining building with locked post office boxes.

Events in Other Counties of Virginia Effect Kingston Parish of Gloucester County—Now Mathews County

"Only a virtuous people are capable of freedom."
Benjamin Franklin

Slaves were ordered to take mail from one plantation to another before 1865. However, during the days when Mathews' County citizens fetched their overland mail from Gloucester, documentation proves trustworthy slaves did long overland hauls. Patricia Perkinson of Topping, Virginia, has been kind in permitting me to use a typed copy of a handwritten petition made by her great-great-great-grandfather, Judge Churchill Blakey. (Judge, Middlesex County). The original petition is in the Virginia State Archives:

PETITION OF HANNAH THACKER LORIMER AND THOMAS FAUNTLEROY AND DIVERS CITIZENS OF THE COMMONWEALTH OF VIRGINIA-REGARDING THE EMANCIPATION OF "SAM" AFTER HIS COURAGE ON NOVEMBER 17, 1797

To the honorable Speaker and members of the House of Delegates of the commonwealth of Virginia-

The petition of Hannah Thacker Lorimer and Thomas Fauntleroy and divers citizens of the commonwealth of Virginia respectfully shew? that James Henry Thacker Lorimer of the County of Middlesex, an infant under the age of twenty-one years and orphan of George Lorimer, dec'd, is possessed of a Negro slave named "Sam" as his absolute property, who was employed for the purpose of conveying public mail from Fredericksburg to Gloucester Courthouse, some time about the 17th day of November 1797, as your petitioners have good reason to believe, and was attacked on the public highway by two persons who attempted to dispossess him of the said mail, but the said Sam with the utmost fortitude and intrepidity resisted the attack until he was relieved from the violence offered by the said persons by some other persons who casually discovered the _____ inconsequence of which resistance and a faithful adherence regard to the trust reposed in him the said slave received several dangerous wounds and languished under them for a considerable space of time thereafter; that many of the citizens of this Commonwealth disposed and _____ to reward the integrity and fortitude of said slave by emancipation and to that end would most willingly pay to his owner the value of said slave by voluntary contributions and your petitioners Hannah T. Lorimer, who is the mother of James H. T. Lorimer, and your petitioner Thomas Faultleroy, who intermarried with the only sister of said James H. T. Lorimer, who hath no brother living, not only wish that the said slave could be emancipated, but would perform any reasonable act to accomplish the same, but as the said James is an infant under the age of twenty-one years and incapable to perform any act which would be requisite for that purpose, your petitioners are advised that the said slave cannot be emancipated without the interposition of the legislature; therefore your petitioners pray that an act may be passed to emancipate the said slave on the payment of such sum of money to the guardian of said James as may be ascertained to be the value of said slave in such a manner as your honorable body may direct or that such mode for his emancipation may be adopted as may be thought most reasonable and consistent with the interest of the proprietor and you petitioners will pray-

Twenty-two signatures: Churchill Blakey. (Judge Middlesex County) is the first signature.

How much of the mail that Sam carried was addressed to someone in Mathews County we will never know. But one must be thankful for such a faithful slave, doing the duty entrusted to him. Sam deserved freedom but as to whether the legislature acted, we have found no record.

National Changes Brings More Mail from Longer Distances

"Night Mail"

"This is the Night Mail crossing the Border,
Bringing the cheque and the postal order,
Letters for the rich, letters for the poor,
The shop at the corner, the girl next door,
Pulling up at Beattock, a steady climb:
The gradient's against her, but she's on time.
Past cotton' grass and moorland border,
Shoveling steam over her shoulder."

W. H. Auden 1936

Both businessmen and the United States Government sought ways for faster delivery of the mail by the early nineteenth century. The country had wider boundaries as men moved westward, finally to the coastline of the Pacific Ocean, requiring more efficient delivery than horseback and stagecoaches. The businessmen experimented with iron and wooden cars, running on rails and pulled with dray horses. They made the first test on the Baltimore and Ohio rails that covered a 13-mile stretch. However by 1830, America's first steam locomotive came on the scene, bringing greater efficiency. Progress moved fast so by July 1838, the United

States legislature passed an Act, designating all the United States as post routes. Thus mail service increased.

Parcel Post began in the late 1800's, but it became law that parcels could be sent in 1912 with services beginning January 1, 1913. With this service official, supporters in all parts of the country celebrated by mailing thousands of parcels in just a few days' time.

In the Midwest during pre-World War I days, children were mailed from one town to the other until the government banned the practice. Postage was much cheaper than train fare since children went for the same rate as a box of chickens. When a mother in Indiana lost custody of her baby during a bitter divorce suit in 1914, she placed the little one in a container and marked it "Live Baby." It required 17 cents postage, mailing it from Stillwell to South Bend. Postal workers made sure of the baby's safe delivery.

When someone reported to USPS that a four-year-old child had been mailed across the state of Idaho, the practice soon ended. The girl traveled for 53 cents. She rode in the mail car with postage stamps attached to her coat, and a mail clerk safely delivered her. When word of her journey reached the Post Office Department, it prompted them to forbid sending any human being by mail. (Facts gleamed from: "Neither Rain nor Snow..." *American History* December 1997))

Two years after the government banned mailing humans, a firm dismantled and shipped an entire bank from Salt Lake, Utah, to Vernal, California. The shipper dismantled 80,000 bricks and shipped them in 50-pound lots. The post office saved the owners money, but both mail agents and railroad workers suffered back strain and untold headaches. After this incident, the postmaster general decreed that no one person could ship over 200 pounds a day.

In the twenty first century we can't conceive of life without parcel post, and present laws and technology forbid ridiculous mailings made in the earlier years of the past century. Yet the post office department has to watch for scams, chain letters and even letters or parcels, containing biological chemicals, in our modern world.

Mail Order Houses Established

"This Book tells just what your storekeeper at home pays for everything he buys and will prevent him from overcharging you on anything you buy from him." Cover of "Fall 1900 Sears Roebuck and Co." Catalog

It was Montgomery Ward, who saw a way to increase sales through parcel post. So the company pioneered, having the first mail-order house in 1872 with a one-page catalog. Montgomery Ward mailed 300 million parcels the first six months of their mail order business. They operated out of Baltimore, where they loaded on the Baltimore and Ohio railroad and steamboats. The steamers carried mail with other freight, pouring from docks on the easternmost area of the city. They traveled down the Chesapeake Bay and stopped at rural communities along their route. Mathews County had many wharfs, where more than one of these steamboats made port of call, most of them supporting a post office: Hicks Wharf, Traders, Williams Wharf, Mobjack, and Fitchetts Wharf among them. Callis Wharf on Gwynns Island delivered to Gwynn Post office after 1900, and mail for Cobbs Creek was dropped off at Green Point and carried to the post office. (Post offices mentioned that we haven't visited will appear in Chapter Three.)

Sears, Roebuck and Company opened their mail-order business in Chicago, Illinois, in 1893. In 1897, after one year of rural delivery from their catalog, Sears boasted they sold four suits and a watch every minute, a revolver every two minutes, and a buggy every ten minutes. After five years shipping by parcel post, Sears had tripled their sales.

Railroads added to their efficiency in deliveries from Chicago.

The mail-order catalog became the most important book in our rural households next to the Bible. It was "The Wish Book," from which the residents chose both needs and wants. They found items the general store had never carried. Therefore they ordered from the catalog that opened a whole new world to many, who had never visited a city.

A monumental medley of goods from catalogs has come and still comes to the county by parcel post: Nurseries mailed trees, plants and bulbs; baby chickens, turkeys and ducklings came through the mail from hatcheries; other items both large and small come from the catalogs that fill mail boxes. Larger items were shipped as freight by steamboats until the mid nineteen thirties. Later railroads delivered the pieces to a terminal in the nearest cities, and trucks completed the delivery.

Daddy ordered baby chickens in lots of 100 by parcel post in the mid-1930s through World War II. They came in boxes, usually holding 25 chicks, with tiny holes covering the top and sides. The chicks created a noise and odor in the store where the post office occupied the front right corner, requiring extra shelf space beyond the post office area. Therefore when he expected the shipment, we had to check for mail daily.

The day the peeping-yellow balls of fuzz arrived, Daddy hitched the wagon and fetched them. It was usually still cool weather so before he left home, the brooder stove had to be lit in the chicken house, and I had the water jars to clean and fill. Bags of mash (a powdered chicken feed for baby chicks) sat in the corner beyond the fine wire that he had stretched around the space allocated for the chickens. The first task when he arrived home was opening the sticky boxes and checking to see if any chicks had died while traveling. After we removed those if they were found, Daddy turned the boxes on their sides and one by one, the chickens slowly stretched their legs for the first time in days. Usually we waited until morning for the first feeding.

As late as 2001, a Hallieford resident in Mathews County, Virginia, heard a loud ruckus in the mailbox cluster near her home. Upon investigation, one large box contained baby turkeys that a neighbor had ordered from a catalog to come parcel post.

Today catalogs fill the mailboxes in Mathews County Post Offices several times a week, and patrons daily leave the post offices with bundles of merchandise ordered from catalogs. In the twenty-first century, Mathews remains a rural area without stoplights, but the homes sit closer together and the farmland has grown smaller than in earlier years. Though the schools have more students than previously, the county is considered a retirement community. And most of these folk enjoy their catalogs, doing relaxed shopping at home. While gathering my mail in 2003, another woman sorted hers, throwing away what she considered "junk." She commented, "I don't know what I'd do without my catalogs. That's how I shop."

RFD Reaches Most Farm Country but Not Mathews

"One good word can warm the heart three months." Japanese proverb

Although informative sources don't mention it, families living in many small rural areas, especially farmlands on the western side of the Chesapeake Bay, still visit the post office to post outgoing letters or parcels and collect their mail from locked boxes. A large percentage of Mathews County residents come under this category. Highway Carriers deliver to the other residents on Star Routes, either with a mailbox at their gate or a cluster of mailboxes at the entrance to a group of homes.

RFD wasn't introduced to other parts of the country until 1893. And though the funds had been appropriated, it took some years to put it in force. Unlike Mathews, where a post office sat every few miles, they had to travel as much as a day's journey to reach the nearest post office. Therefore they made weekly or monthly excursions for food, supplies and their mail. Remember, there were no telephones, radios or televisions back then so mail was their only connection with the outside world.

RFD was virtually impossible before the introduction of the gummed stamp in 1855 in England because recipients paid postage on the receiver's end. Since all mail came COD, the mail carrier had to see someone, who could pay on delivery. When RFD began, the mailman placed each household's mail in the mailbox they furnished with their box number inscribed. The carrier probably didn't know the people. RFD continues today in the farm belt. But only a portion of Mathews County residents receive mail delivered by the Highway Carrier on Star Routes. (Most facts gleaned from *History of United States Postal System 1775-1993*)

Picture courtesy *Gloucester-Mathews Gazette-Journal*

Inside Moon Post Office and general merchandise store on a cold blustery day in winter during the 1950s.

Chapter Three

Fitchetts Post Office Established in 1880

"But words are things, and a small drop of ink, falling like dew upon a thought, produces that which makes thousands, perhaps, millions, think." Lord Byron

Today a sign at the entrance of Route 642, Fitchetts Wharf Road, tells the history of the wharf William Fitchett, known as "Tip," had built over the deep waters of Milford Haven. When one drives down the road approaching the location, homes sit in manicured yards and many sparkle with fresh coats of paint or siding. The landscaping is unlike the period when this area, known as Field Neck, was first occupied. Back then, either picket or rail fences with several wooden gates enclosed the yards. Cows, horses and sometimes sheep did the mowing. Fowl of various species and colors pecked among and behind the animals. My daddy would have nothing except Rhode Island Red chickens while Dick Landon, who lived across the road declared his White Legons the best for his egg business. The architecture of a few houses on this road dates the buildings to the nineteenth or early twentieth centuries. While some older edifices are plain and unadorned, the façade of others tell they date from the Victorian age. In the past few decades, the waterfront has become lined with new homes. I grew up in Field Neck, and I am amazed at the number of new houses on the waters edge. Some on land that Daddy farmed for those no longer physically able to keep it from growing into brushwood.

Reaching the end of the road, the path to the right of where the wharf once sat has been blocked. One can only park to one side and walk around the locked gate to the shell path where wagons and buggies drove for many years, and afterwards trucks and automobiles continued to crush the shells. Many residents, including my family walked this wide path through the years that Fitchetts Post Office, the store and wharf operated.

In the earlier years of the neck's development, Lewis Hudgins had one of the largest shipyards in the state, reaching its height of production in 1845 before Fitchett built his wharf. The Northern troops burned the shipyard in 1864 during the Civil War. Back then local settlers had named this peninsula "Field Neck". It sat between Billups Creek to the east and Stutts Creek to the northwest. Both creeks are wide and large, having an average depth of 10 to 12 feet at the shore. Lillys Neck on the south and Point Breeze to the north stretch toward one another at the mouth of Milford Haven with the Chesapeake Bay beyond. The two peninsulas provide protection from stormy weather. Thus it offered a safe place for ships to moor, as well as, the perfect location for a shipyard.

The most famous ship that Hudgins built was the "Victoria" in 1849. The 114-foot ship boasted three masts and could carry 317 tons, according to the information given a *Gloucester-Mathews Gazette Journal* reporter by his great-great grandson, Robert Hudgins. His shipyard sat to the left of the shell road that leads to the wharf. The location is just back of the fine late-nineteenth-century home owned by Keith Lowe, but originally built by Haywood Hudgins according to J. T. Godwin, whose grandparents lived down the lane opposite Lowe's place. Lewis had a dock, but conflicting stories do not allow me to pinpoint where it sat. Some say to the side of the shipyard and others feel where Fitchett later built his wharf.

The once affluent ship builder's large unadorned home still stands far to the right, now accessible only by a lane before one reaches the gate, going to the wharf. He and his two wives are buried in the small fenced family cemetery on the way to his home. Other members of the Hudgins family are buried in the same graveyard with just room for one to step between the graves. The owners of both the house and cemetery properties, with a member of the Hudgins family assisting, keep the place in top shape.

Hudgins had built a general merchandise store beyond his yard in front of the cemetery. Today, it sits within a large updated house, which has large windows on the waterfront entrance. The floors of the store that were once practically black from the hundreds of coats of oil applied to the surface for cleaning purposes glow as only rich pine-heart flooring can. The house faces the water rather than the private shell road like the store did.

William E. and Mary Catherine Fitchett (friends and neighbors knew the couple as "Tip" and "Puss") first owned the Victorian house on the right side of the shell-covered road when approaching the location where the wharf and store had sat. Today, James and Sarah Jo Whitten own the Fitchett home. Their dock is near the location where Fitchett's Wharf, which has rotted away, once sat. Over time waves have gnawed away the wharf's pilings that stood for years after the wharf vanished. I remember, spending many Sunday afternoons in the forties with my fiancé and later my husband, sitting on the edge of the old wharf. While we talked of his experiences in the Navy and future plans and dreams, we skipped shells, watching the waters ripple. Sweet memories often dispel loneliness today and urge me to delve into more history.

Tradition says Lewis Hudgins gave "Tip" Fitchett the land for his house and wharf before the sale of the property to a Mr. Borum. Some believe Fitchett ranked high in position, operating some part of Hudgins' enterprises. Fitchett married Mary Catherine James, whose family originally lived on the upper portion of Stutts Creek. The Fitchett family lived in the Victorian house, as early as the beginning of the third quarter of the nineteenth century. As to whether Hudgins built it before the Civil War, or Fitchett did the building afterwards is uncertain. Since Mary Catherine James Fitchett's grandfather built the house, in which I was born and spent my first 22 years, for members of the Lewis Hudgins family, perhaps Grandpa James built his granddaughter's house. A small community grew at this bustling point, where sloops with their tall sails made deliveries and picked up freight—lumber being the larger export.

By 1879, William E. Fitchett who had built and operated the wharf and warehouse, saw need for a post office. So he applied to the Post Office Department, receiving appointment in March 1880. The small building that housed the post office for some years sat across the road from the Fitchett home. Mary Catherine, or "Puss," acted as postmaster during the years "Tip" held the position according to her niece and nephews, Frank Davis from Mathews, Wilson Davis from Mobjack and Roberta Davis Huey from Maryland and Mobjack. The post office sat on the outside edge of the property on which Haywood Hudgins had built his house. Across the road, Sarah Jo Whitten brings beauty to her yard with an enclosed herb garden like those of yesteryear in Williamsburg, Virginia. It's a garden that "Puss" Fitchett would have been proud, placed near where Aunt Mandy's shack sat in my early childhood. Fitchett hired Aunt Mandy, the daughter of a slave, and let her live on in the shack where she had spent her childhood. Evidently that is where she felt at home.

In conversations with Harriet Smith Farmer and Joicie Smith Davis they both spoke of their dad, Seabrook Smith, working in the small post office on the side of the road. Since his name doesn't appear in the National Archives, he was an assistant.

Originally Fitchett's Post Office appeared as the name. But the Washington D.C. Archives show it was changed when William E. Fitchett became postmaster for the second time in September 1893, leaving out the apostrophe.

However, "Fitchett's Wharf" is still used. The wharf and warehouse were essential for freight delivered by the Baltimore-based sloops and later steamboat lines that ran along the western shore of the Chesapeake Bay as well as Fitchett's retail business. This was their southernmost port of call.

The steamboat didn't bring just freight and passengers, but also the mail from the north for both "Field Neck" and "The Haven" residents and Mathews Post Office. Then the boat traveled to other ports of call on Milford Haven and up the Piankatank River to several Mathews County ports of call, ending at Freeport Landing, Gloucester County. At this last port, it completely emptied its cargo hold and the last passengers left their staterooms for a stay in the country, or to journey into the county, taking orders for Baltimore Companies. The officers and crew spent the night at Freeport, either in the accommodations above the post office and store or aboard the boat. Baltimore salesmen had no other way to reach storeowners in the area, but by steamboat. After arriving, they rented a room and a horse and buggy to travel to business locations. This was repeated at Fitchetts another week.

The next morning the crew reloaded at all ports of call. The cargo hold held lumber, oysters, and country produce, according to a billhead from W. E. Fitchett that Gerald W. Morgan has in his possession. And the captain or other official loaded the outgoing mail in its bag. (Tradition and newspaper articles tell us this was true at all ports of call.) An official gathered mailbags, adding them to the freight. Then passengers boarded after deck hands completed loading. It was near noon before they reached Fitchett's Wharf to load the last outgoing freight and mail, picking up anyone ready to board for the return trip home or a visit in the city. Baltimore was the center of trade on the Bay until after the turn of the twentieth century when Norfolk became an active city. Since the steamer made two trips a week, passengers could choose their stay as desired.

While searching for pictures in the files of the *Gloucester-Mathews Gazette-Journal* Archives, I found a letterhead of a two-page letter, dated June 1887 that William E. Fitchett had mailed to a business associate in Norfolk. On the line below Fitchett's name, it read: "Dealer in Lath, Lime, Brick, Hardware, Paints, Oils, Varnishes, Sc, Sc," He operated his business from the Wharf.

During its latter years, the post office moved to the general store, operated by Franklin P. Callis, who was postmaster from February 1923 until July 1929. At that time, he became the assistant to his elder son, Howard F. Callis, who served as postmaster until April 1930. Later Frank Callis assisted Bertram Lee Owens for a short time during Owens five years as postmaster.

I walked a quarter mile to the general-merchandise store in warm weather as early as four-years-old, carrying letters to mail on some trips. On other occasions, it was a dozen eggs carried in a tin bucket, lined with cloth, to exchange for groceries or a due bill, always picking up any incoming mail. I preferred going the day the Piankatank Steamboat delivered to see the men unload freight and the young women, dressed in beautiful new ready-made clothing and wearing makeup. They came ashore to stretch their legs and refresh their thirst with a soft drink. They often treated me to sticks of chewing gum or penny pieces of candy, once even a soda, but I enjoyed just giving them my name, age and other little tidbits of information. For in those days one had little touch with the outside world in our rural neighborhood. I fetched the family's mail and sometimes small grocery items before the trek home. Those trips made the mundane exciting days.

Franklin P. Callis' daughter, Olive C. Gwynn, accepted the postmaster's position in March 1935, serving a short period. After her term, an Officer in Charge kept the office, operating until the United States Post Office

Department saw fit to close Fitchetts Post Office in June 1937, and the mail went to Moon Post Office.

When the post office closed, the neighborhood felt it had lost a friend. In the 1940s, the enlarged general-merchandise store became a home with other homes increasing in the surrounding area. Folks enjoyed the waterfront. An automotive vehicle of one sort or another sits in each yard—sometimes two or three. One only walks for health's sake.

Fitchetts Post Office where "Pus" Fitchett served some years as assistant postmaster with her husband, William Fitchett, the official postmaster. Back in 1880, the building had no shutters or light fixture. It looked much like it did in my childhood, stained a dark brownish tone with linseed oil and umber. It has served as a washhouse in the years since it was moved to "Milford" on Stutts Creek shortly after World War II. (Some believe the guesthouse at Keith Lowe's home to have been the post

office. However my research proved that Lewis Hudgins' granddaughter, Eoline Wolfe, paid to have the building moved to "Milford" when Mrs. Fales was going to have it dismantled as she did the icehouse. Then Fales had the quest house built. The timbers in the guest house have been examined, proving they were much newer than 1880, helping to confirm my information.)

Doesn't this county look like nothing but necks, sprouting from the center? I thought. I shook my head for I had never seen it as such earlier. I guess I've been too busy growing to adulthood, helping to establish a home with my late husband, raising children and working to do more than travel these roads without notice of the configuration of the land. The old quotation, "I can't see the trees because I'm too close to the woods," applies here.

Diggs Post Office Became the County's Twelfth

"Letters mingle souls". John Donne

I leave Fitchett's Wharf Road at the intersection and turned left on Haven Beach Road, bypassing Lilly's Neck. I head toward the area known for years as "The Haven," where the Chesapeake Bay borders the beach. Stokes Creek hugs the eastern side of this peninsula, and Whites Creek borders a part of the western side. I head directly towards the Bay, south of that creek. Still farther south a private beach lies on Garden Creek.

Suddenly, I am at the corner where the general store had sat with the post office in the corner many of the years since 1897 until it burnt in 1979. The post office had moved to Nicholas Owens' store on Knight Woods Road in 1923. Postmasters served in the latter location for 39 years. After closing, the Owens building rotted down through the years. Haven Beach Road continues to the left, but I turn right on

Aarons Beach Road to find the new post office site. I leave the empty space, where the store burnt almost a quarter century ago.

It was a *Gloucester-Mathews Gazette Journal* reporter, who researched the original site of Diggs Post Office in 1985, for the original application and the location didn't tie together. Walter F. Diggs applied for a post office in 1881, but the location lay on the opposite shore of Garden Creek near the present Onemo Post Office. He asked for a post office three miles east of East River, a quarter mile west of Winter Harbor and the application read "would be situated in the Chesapeake Township." Walter Diggs wanted the post office that he was about to establish to be called "Winslowville." There had been a Winslow Foster, living in what was known as Bethel, (in the nineteenth century, communities were known by the names of local churches and cemeteries since post offices didn't exist) and near Pear Tree Cemetery (now at Onemo), according to the late Mrs. Cecil Morgan.

Diggs' request for a post office was granted, but the name he gave rejected. So whether the post office was named for the applicant or for the Sam Diggs, who, according to tradition, had the distinction of receiving more mail than anyone else in the community, no one knows. Legend says that the founding fathers considered it only appropriate the post office be named for Sam Diggs.

Walter Diggs's post office was discontinued the end of February 1883, and the mail sent to Port Haywood less than four miles from the present Onemo according to the National Archives. However, they show it operated again in March 1890 with Oscar Hudgins as postmaster.

Oscar Hudgins operated a general merchandise store at the head of Stoakes Creek, on Haven Beach Road and near Knights Woods Road, prior to 1890. With 250 people occupying "The Haven" community, people cried for their own post office. Hudgins requested the name "Haven Post

Office," but the post office department gave the already approved name, "Diggs Post Office." So it just moved across Garden Creek and northwestward.

In 1897, Hugh Hudgins built the largest General Merchandise Store in "The Haven" on the corner where I had paused. That was the same year he received appointment as postmaster. Remember in those days, no one had electricity, telephones, radios or TV, and automobiles were practically unknown. So both the men and women in the neighborhood depended on the community's general merchandise store for all needs: Food the farm didn't produce, fabrics with sewing supplies, clothing they didn't make, pots and pans, men's pocket watches, over the counter medications and farming tools became demands. What the store didn't stock, customers could order from a catalog that sat on the counter. I've found "Baltimore Bargain House" stamped on the back of more than one piece of furniture from the Fitchetts community.

As political parties changed so did most postmasters across the United States in the nineteenth and early twentieth centuries. So others served between Oscar, Hugh and lastly his son Jesse Hudgins, whose term ended in 1923. That was the year Nicholas Owens received appointment, moving the post office to the store that he owned and operated. And a few months later his son, B.L. Owens, became postmaster. Like Trader in the Chapter Two, B.L. Owens was postmaster of Fitchetts Post Office when he accepted this position, proving assistant postmasters did the work in these offices. But the postmaster still carried the responsibility for the reports and finances. Mrs. Clara Owens told that her husband, William E. Owens, worked as assistant postmaster at Diggs when they married in 1928. The National Archives records say his appointment to official postmaster occurred in April 1930, and he remained in office until the end of November 1962. Then Diggs Post Office moved back to the Hudgins' store when Owens retired.

Elwood L. Hudgins, who then owned the store, served as assistant postmaster until his official appointment in January 1964. He served 10 years. It was in 1974 that the post office moved from the store building, which had closed for business, and to a large step van. The "Old Jesse Hudgins" store, as people called it through the years, burnt in 1979.

Other postmasters came and went until Elizabeth Rowe assumed charge in 1983 with 90-some postal patrons. The post office still operated from the step van south of the post office, but three years later it moved to a permanent postal trailer. Since 1987 when Rowe left for a larger post office, many OICs have served. In 2004 Karen Barrick is the OIC with 57 patrons.

Courtesy the *Gloucester-Mathews Gazette-Journal*

Once the pride of the neighborhood, Jessie Hudgins' old store where Diggs Post Office sat for many years, burnt in 1979. Picture taken shortly afterwards.

Life in Field Neck and The Haven

"The greatest pleasure I know is to do a good action by stealth, and to have it found by accident." Charles Lamb

The post offices wouldn't have been needed if more people hadn't settled in the communities during the late nineteenth and early twentieth centuries. People need guidance from above and fellowship with one another, and these were no different. They needed places to worship and schools with staff to teach their children to read, write and do arithmetic, and places for neighborhood meetings besides the stores.

According to a church history prepared by Marguerite R. Sadler: during the eighteenth and nineteenth centuries, people of the area gathered in an old dwelling house to worship. They called the building "Milford Meeting House," and it stood on Route 644, Salem Church Road, near the intersection of Haven Beach Road, and north of where Salem United Methodist Church sits today. In the 1700's the congregation secured another meetinghouse known as "Billups Meeting House." It sat on the corner of Fitchetts Wharf Road and Haven Beach Road. Robert Billups, grandfather of Walter Stoakes, owned the building.

The Methodist Quarterly Conference passed a resolution in 1821 to build a church in Milford Haven. However, it wasn't until some years later that John Forrest, an early superintendent, donated the property for the church building after a near-fatal illness. He had assured friends and relatives, who gathered around his bed, saying: "God has a work for me to do. I am not going to die." By 1855 the first section of the church building was completed and dedicated. Methodist Circuit preachers served as pastors for many generations. The church, known as Salem United Methodist Church, supports a pastor today, and there have been many additions, including a steeple.

The Stoakes family, for whom the creek was named, owned a grand home built about 1620. In the early twentieth century, the community called it "Stoakes famous old place." Walter and his wife, Essie, entertained many visitors from Richmond, whom they brought to Salem Church in their surrey. He even brought his aging mother with her footstool. Walter Stoakes was not only a prominent man in the community, but served under Robert E. Lee in the Confederate Army in the Civil War. Major Giles B. Cooke of Palace Green, Mathews, commanded his battalion. The surviving men had grown close during that war and kept in touch.

Stoakes established a private primer school on the right side of the entrance to his yard. My grandmother attended the school, but she died when she was only 38 so never knew her grandchildren. Though his home is still occupied, the school disappeared years ago.

Milford Haven Elementary Public School for students in Field Neck and The Haven succeeded Stoakes' school with three rooms for the six classes. My daddy attended this school as early as 1908. I attended Milford Haven School my first six years in Mathews County schools, beginning in September 1932. The school was downgraded in the 1938 when the School Board reduced it to three grades. In 1939 it closed its doors, and students attended Lee Jackson, traveling on the school bus. In those days the bus had a long seat on each side with double benches, back to back, running down the middle aisle. If two long legged students faced each other, their knees bumped. All high school students, beginning with the 8th grade attended the new consolidated high school. I graduated as member of the first class, beginning as freshman.

The sturdy one-story-school building, where so many of us had our first schooling, sold easily and was converted into a home. Mrs. Peyton Park occupied it until March 2004. Whether her family will use it as a vacation home or sell it is uncertain at this writing. The home has conveniences that school children didn't enjoy—electricity, running water, a bathroom and baseboard heat. She and her husband were the second owners since the county sold the property. So when I worked in the home, she asked me to point out the classroom partitions. I found that a simple task.

The community erected the Community Hall sometime after they built the school on a lot, adjoining the school property. The students performed plays and holiday programs in the hall through the school years. Some remember: "Little Harry of the Revolution," "Poor Married Man" and "The Womanless Wedding." After a performance closed, the men brought in a favorite treat for all ages in those days--freezers of homemade ice cream, still packed, with old quilts wrapped around them, to keep them cold. Once opened, the women reached for large scoops (unlike most of today's, they held a cup), putting the rich delicacy into bowls and charging a nickel each. Other women uncovered cakes with their knives ready to cut slices for those preferring cake or wanting both if they had two nickels or a dime. Sometimes instead of ice cream and cake, they had pie socials when older groups performed in the hall. A large slice of pie would be a dime. This and on occasions the low admittance charges was their means of supporting the maintenance of the Community Hall. It stands on the property and is used for storage today.

Weather played a big role in the mail carriers' travels, especially in "The Haven." Anyone, living on or near the Chesapeake Bay, is familiar with rains, winds and tides. In higher elevations, such weather is just a storm—usually in spring or fall. But when nor'easters hit the county, the mail carrier had to be prepared to unhitch his horse and ride horseback with the mailbag held high, traveling through tide to reach Diggs Post Office. He would remember the Motto on the New York Post Office. *"Neither snow nor rain nor heat nor gloom of night stays these carriers from swift completion of their appointed rounds."* As Maxine Morgan Crockett called it "lo', po' land," when talking to the *Gloucester-Mathews Gazette-Journal* reporter. Deep salt waters often covered Haven Beach Road for a good distance. But if at all possible, the mail went through safely.

"Hookemfair" Became Hudgins

"The world likes a good loser, particularly if it gets some of his money."(Chicago Ledger September 1933)

Six miles north of Mathews Court House in about 1883, William N. Trader, an industrious entrepreneur, and a partner, either Thomas Hudgins or John Dixon, occupied the new building in the hamlet where Hudgins lived. The men manufactured crocks, used in every household's kitchen, and even smoke houses for salted fish. According to the inscription on the existing crooks, they also stocked stoves and furniture. Having accumulated enough inventory to stock the store, they planned to open the business to customers on the day they had already announced. The partner said to Trader, "tomorrow we'll hook 'em." Trader replied, "Yes we'll hook 'em but we'll hook them fair." After the conversation they named their business "Hookemfair." (Quotes from the *Gloucester-Mathews Gazette-Journal*)

John Dixon ran the store, which occupied part of the building. A post office cage sat in the corner where the merchandise occupied space, and mail was delivered and picked up. There is no record of who applied for the post office—Dixon or Trader, but we know they asked it be "Hookemfair Post Office." The National Archives gives Hudgins from its beginning in May 1883. However, the people interviewed in the 1980's tell us it operated as Hookemfair Post Office until it moved south to the intersection of Route 198, Buckley Hall Road, and Route 223, Cricket Hill Road.

John Dixon's grandson, John W. Dixon, speaks about his Grandfather Dixon serving as postmaster at Hookemfair. So like many other post offices, mail deliveries had been made before the appointment became official in Washington D. C.

Thomas "Brass" Hudgins ran a general merchandise store opposite Trader's store to the south, but it was been built later than Trader's building. Clarence Hudgins was the first postmaster recorded in the National Archives, and since the post office department often used the name of the applicant, it seems that either Thomas or Clarence submitted the final application. An elderly woman of the 1980s, Mrs. Mary Pusey Smith, had lived in the area her lifetime, and she affirmed that Thomas Hudgins' store was built after Traders. It moved when postmasters changed due to political parties shifting. Trader was a Republican and Hudgins was a Democrat. So if they were partners, they split over politics. John Dixon ran Trader's store after he died, and they worked together before his death. Thankfully, changes in parties have not effected who serves as postmaster in many decades.

There were three Thomas Hudgins in the area so it became necessary to make a distinction between them. Thomas "Brass" Hudgins was quite deaf and used a big brass horn to amplify sound thus acquired his nickname. Mrs. Sadie Billups, 103 years old in 1983 when she talked to a *Gloucester-Mathews Gazette-Journal* reporter, chuckled as she told this story. She had already told what a stately and tall man he was. However, there was "Long Tom" Hudgins at Port Haywood and another Thomas known as "Coffeepot" Hudgins of Mathews.

About 1905, Ulysses G. Dillehay, known as U.G., built his large general merchandise store, with a long two-story house adjoining the back, just south of Mathews Baptist Church, which dated to 1779. With other exiting businesses at this busy corner, Hudgins Post Office moved to Dillehay's store. He became postmaster in March 1919 and held the position until his retirement in May 1945. He lived three more years while Alice Dillehay, U.G.'s second and much younger wife, filled the position of postmaster until May 1956. Alice changed the old fashioned store to a self-service market, giving her time to accomplish her post office duties while she operated the business.

If you have never visited an old-fashioned general merchandise store, let's take a tour. One carried their memorandum, calling out one item after another to the storekeeper After each item, he went to the stocked shelves or barrel in case of weighed or measured items, pulling them and placing the item on the counter in front of you. Sometimes the canned goods sat on shelves far beyond the storekeeper's reach, having stocked them from a ladder. He used a long handled grabber that fit around a can to take it from the shelf and down to his reach. The grabber hung on a hook attached to an upright divider. Barrels contained molasses and vinegar, for which you needed to have brought jars or a jug. Large sacks of flour and sugar or salt often sat in barrels that had been emptied of other goods. The storekeeper just scooped the product from the cloth bag into a paper one. Nothing came prepackaged as it does today, but needed to be measured or weighed and placed in a sack. If the store stocked a full general merchandise line as Dillehay had in the beginning, he pulled and measured fabric, got thread from a spool cabinet, pulled the piece of clothing or toy that you selected. No one shopped swiftly on busy days the family or hired help assisted him. But there would only be one moneybox and later a hand-operated cash register. Customers usually didn't mind the wait since it gave time to browse and look at the counter catalogue. Practically every general merchandise store had gas tanks in front after 1920 when more and more of the population traveled in automobiles.

In an interview with Dillehay's younger son, John Dillehay, whose mother was Alice, I learned he was born in an upstairs room of the house. The family lived in the two-story home for some years, dividing it into two apartments later. They lived in one and rented the other. John had older half siblings by his father's first wife with children his age. In fact a nephew older than John Dillehay, John W. Dixon, tells of days that he played with young Dillehay in the back of the store and in both floors of the house. His parents happened to be one of the renters after Dillehay divided the house into apartments so the boys grew up to be very close in their childhood.

Alice Dillehay retired from postmaster, continuing to operate the self-service store, in 1956 so the post office moved across Buckley Hall Road to a building owned by Wilton and Mary Dunton. Their son, Wilton E. (Bud) Dunton, Jr., served as postmaster for thirty-one years, retiring in 1987. Upon his retirement, Nora K. Diggs became the new postmaster and serves still in 2004.

Hudgins, as the area is known, has the oldest and largest Baptist Church in the county at its center. It is often referred to as "Old Baptist." The church has had many improvements through the years so the earlier members probably wouldn't even recognize it today.

In the late 1930s, Wilton ("Donk") and Mary Dunton purchased the home with a large yard on the left corner lot across from Mathews Baptist Church. They moved to the county with their two children, Jacqueline, known as "Jackie," and Wilton Jr., called "Bud." The Duntons built a service station, selling Gulf® gasoline and other of the company's products. Inside the small store, they provided self-service snacks and staples. I learned when I interviewed their son-in-law, Conrad Rowe, that they made two additions because it became such a popular gathering place for the youth of the county. Mary made sandwiches; they served soft drinks, chips, ice cream and other things the young folks enjoyed while with their peers. The jukebox played the latest hit songs while some of the youth mingled their voices. Donks was just a clean place for Mathews County's youth to have fun.

By the mid forties with World War II over, "Donk" and Mary felt the county needed a theater to keep local people from having to travel long distances for entertainment. The Be-Jo Theater in Mathews Court House had closed during the war because of lack of attendance.

Donk's Theater showed their first picture on June 9, 1947 in what was the largest commercial building in Mathews County. The theater could seat 504 people on soft, upholstered seats, having the latest equipment available to show movies. Times continued to change with more residents owning automobiles and traveling out of the county, making it necessary to post a closing date of October 3, 1970. "Nashville Music" was the last feature shown.

Jimmy Smith and his wife, Carolyn, passed the empty theater every Sunday on their way to church. After returning from a trip to Nashville, Tennessee, where they attended *The Grand Ole Opry*, he kept looking at the vacant building, housing the auditorium. Finally, he suggested what he had been thinking. "What a great place for a small Old Opry." It was the beginning. Two of Jimmy's older sisters had already made a name for themselves as "The Smith Girls" act on the radio and at other popular locations. The family agreed to contact the Duntons, who gladly rented the building. They began their own "Virginia's Lil Ole Opry'," organizing as Wickham Enterprises. The first show opened on June 14, 1975 with a packed house.

The Smith's home at "Field Point" sat across a small creek, my dad called a cove, from my parents' home. So I grew up aware of their talent. Many a Saturday night in summer and early fall, with lights out, windows open next to the cove and the rest of my family in bed, I sat, listening as the family sang country western music around a bonfire. The aroma of burning logs drifted into my room if the wind blew the right way. I'd see cinders flying in the air as someone stirred the fire, perhaps adding a log. The guitars drummed on, and then they began another song, someone yodeling many times before it ended. Little did the group know they had an audience. I enjoyed the unrehearsed performance more than Nashville's *Grand Old Opry* on the radio. After Jimmy and Carolyn married, they sang in church services and at public functions in Mathews.

Wickham Enterprises brought in talent from Northern Neck, Middlesex, Gloucester, New Kent, Norfolk, Richmond and areas in-between and beyond. They have featured stars the likes of Ernest Tubb, Mickey Gilley, Kitty Wells, Dolly Parton, and others. New stars have performed for the first time on Donk's stage. At first they opened two or three weeks out of a month. But now, Virginia's "Lil Ole Opry'" presents a live show every Saturday night from spring until the Christmas family show in December. (Information from my experience, plus interviews and facts in *History and Progress, Mathews County, Virginia* published by MCHS)

In the twenty-first century Dillehay could be proud of the small business district in which he built his general merchandise store, adding the post office. The post office, with its own entrance sits next to the theater in a mini-strip mall, and a church group worships on the opposite side; the "Blue Heron", a gift shop, occupies the Dillehay building; Donks' original building has become a florist; Frank Crittenden and Bobby Diggs offer top line lawn mowers with service at Chimney Corner Lawnmower, Inc.; one doesn't go to Hughes Planing Mill to have lumber dressed, but to purchase building supplies though the original Hughes are no longer on the scene,but son Robert manages the business; Zooms, a convenience store, sits on the right corner across from Mathews Baptist Church, which has been enlarged; and by Zooms on Cricket Hill Road; I go to Dr. Paul Edwards' office for eye exams and new eye glasses, parking in the ample parking lot. Past the church and a couple houses, I buy gasoline from Dixon's, which now joins Wroten Oil, Inc. A few years my senior, Bill Dixon, who is another grandson of U. G. Dillehay, still offers the service he did back in the 1950s when I visited the station with my sister. He not only pumps gas, but picks up his glass cleaner and a cloth, cleaning windshields, and he'll ask to check under the hood if he hadn't done it recently—services we took for granted in past years.

The post office still operates in the building owned by the Dunton descendents. The assistant postmaster reports in December 2004 that 308 of the 418 post office boxes are rented. The office services 88 Star Route customers.

Hookemfair Post Office sat in the corner of the original two-story building before moving across the road and later to Hudgins. It is now the American Legion Building.

It would relieve me if the postman would leave a letter from you." (Post Card 1916)

Hudgins Post Office--where the post office sat in a corner from about 1905 when it moved from Hookemfair until 1956 is on the front corner. U.G. Dillehay built the store with the large family home attached.

Chapter Four

Mail Carriers Span Milford Haven

Gwynn's Post Office Established

"A wholesome tongue is a tree of life." Proverbs 15:4

Today, the Coast Guard Station sits west of the location where Cricket Hill Post Office once sat, and the approach to the bridge to Gwynn's Island is west of the CGS. Instead of a rowboat, canoe or ferry, one drives over the 723 feet 3inches of concrete surface, forming a pivot pier bridge with a 204-foot swing span. There is only one hitch: The span opens frequently in warm weather to allow pleasure boats, with mastheads or fly towers more than 14 feet tall, to pass. The only two stoplights in Mathews County sit at either end of the bridge, stopping traffic when the swing span opens. Since this occurs many times a day in summer to let vacationers through, one must be prepared to stop—a good time to enjoy watching the boaters and sea gulls.

In an interview with Eugene Ripley, a bridge attendant, he said that the bridge opens little in the winter months with few oysters and clams left to harvest. Pollution and disease have taken their toll on the industries that once supported most residents. There are still a few clam boats, according to Ripley. But when working in summer, he keeps busy from early morning, opening the bridge to let pleasure boats through.

Tradition tells of the day that the Indian maiden Pocohontas, daughter of the powerful Chief Powhatan, almost drowned while boating in the Pianatank River. Hugh Gwynn saw the fair maiden struggling after her boat capsized in the stormy waters. Rowing to her location, he and his two accompanying slaves rescued Pocohontas, who gave him the nearby island in gratitude. From that time it became known as Gwynn's Island. Though he still lived on the mainland, England officially granted him one third of the island some 30 years later in 1640. He cleared land and built his log home, moving his family there in 1643. Gwynn named the body of water that his home faced "Milford Haven" after a similar spot in Wales.

Gwynn traveled the seas, as did Captain George Keeble and Captain George Reade, who also received original grants from England for the land on Gwynn's Island—each owning one third of the total. They brought other settlers to the colonies and thus to the island, receiving grants from the original recipients. When the children grew to adulthood, the sons tied the families together by marrying one of the daughters of the other grant holders. But they grew, not only in numbers, but also in sir names: Hudgins, Brooks, Callis, Carney and more. Since most of the colonists near the coast traveled by boat, these residents did not consider themselves isolated. Peter Jennings Wrike noted in his book, *The Governors' Island*, that by 1700 there were fifty inhabitants on the island, including African-Americans and white indentured servants. He added: "Gwynn's Island residents lived comfortably."

When Governor Dunmore invaded the island in May 1776, most families reluctantly fled to the mainland. Dunmore's fleet destroyed all property except the Keeble house during and at the end of their occupancy. Some returned to rebuild while others moved to various parts of the mainland.

Many families inhabited Gwynn's Island by the mid nineteenth century, and their descendents continue to make it their residence in the twenty-first century. But those folk back then had to enjoy the water that surrounded them and the rural atmosphere. There was no bridge and not even a ferry until the year 1884 according to *History and Progress --Mathews, County, Virginia, 1949* taken from the *Mathews-Gloucester Gazette-Journal.* They rowed across the narrowest body of water to Cricket Hill to fetch their mail, but longed for their own post office.

Gwynn's Post Office first operated in May 1883 with Lucie J. Powell as postmaster. So the mail carrier sculled a canoe or skiff from Cricket Hill with the horse swimming behind, landing at Narrows Point. If there was no horse-drawn conveyance for him to use, he rode horseback, carrying the mailbag to and from the post office as earlier riders had done—only they used saddlebags. Thankfully, before the year ended, the first ferry service became available.

Thomas E. Edwards told when he was 11 years old, the citizens of Gwynn's Island and the mainland decided that a ferry should be instituted. To raise funds, in the summer of 1883, they had a big dinner under oak trees near where Gwynn's Post Office sits today. The proceeds allowed finances for the ferry service. A group of local men took stock in the organization that had been formed to maintain the service. They carried a steel cable, atop several poles, across the water from Cricket Hill to Narrows Point, enabling one to pull the ferry across.

"About ten years later, when I was 21 years," said Edwards, "I took the job of ferryman for about a month. I was paid $12 for it and it was the hardest work I ever did in my life. We had a wooden device with which we gripped the cable, and I would walk to the front of the boat, then grab this wood on the cable and walk all the way to the back. In other words we made just one boat length every time I pulled. ..." (Reference from *History and Progress, Mathews County, Virginia,* published by MCHS)

The fare amounted to 25 cents a round trip for riding on the small flatboat with rails on each side that only carried two or three horse-drawn conveyances. However, Edwards carried passengers with no vehicles across in his skiff for a nickel. We wonder: Why hadn't someone thought of the service years before? It would have enabled residents to fetch their mail from Cricket Hill more easily.

Sometime later, when gasoline engines powered boats, the ferryman used a small inboard five horsepower engine boat, attached alongside the ferry to take it across. In about 1925, another ferry traveled from Callis Wharf to New Cricket Hill. The privately owned barge, like the first ferry, used a chock that was connected to a cable to pull it across. A larger lighter with a powerboat lashed to its side replaced the hand powered ferry. Then ferries became available with their own engines. The late Eleanor Respress, known on the island as "Miss Eleanor," told a *Gloucester-Mathews Gazette Journal* reporter that in 1883 her father, James Thomas Powell, had traveled to Norfolk to purchase the first motorized ferry. By this time the county had become responsible for the conveyance. So Powell approached the board of supervisors for a larger ferry "until we get a bridge."

Board members laughed at him, thinking they would never build a bridge over Milford Haven. Captain Powell operated the new vessel, carrying both vehicles and passengers, until a captain could be found to do the job. Until it was paid for, the car and driver were 25 cents and each passenger 5 cents. Then the fee was reduced to a flat 25 cents with any number of passengers, and finally all rides were free. The state took over the ferry service in the 1930s, and then built the bridge. With the building of the toll-free bridge in 1939, all ferry service ceased.

Through these years of progress in accessing Gwynn's Island, the post office continued to operate, though it moved from time to time. However, the name became Gwynn Post Office in March 1902.

I interviewed a smartly dressed and stately woman named Gazelle Moore in Mathews Convalescent Center in 2004. She talked of the past with excitement from her wheel chair. Ninety-five-year-old Gazelle Hudgins Moore, known to many as "Toody," was born and raised on the island. She was still unattached when Gwynn's Baptist Church acquired a single pastor. A courtship developed between the two, and they married before he left for pastorate to another church. They moved several times before his death at age 39. Then Mrs. Moore worked in the Baptist Home in Richmond, Virginia, until her retirement 30 years ago. At that time, she moved back to the Island that was home to her and lived a full life until some months previous to my interview.

Moore stated that post offices had always been in the corner of a store on Gwynn's Island before remembering that when Marcellus J. Booze became postmaster in February 1912, the post office had moved. It sat in a small building across from the hotel on Haven Drive. He lived in a room of the hotel. So when that burnt little more than two years after he became postmaster, Booze resigned, having to find new living quarters.

It was Moore's grandfather, John M. Carney, who owned a store on Old Ferry Road in 1897, when he became Gywnn's postmaster. Later her father, John Rosser Hudgins, also operated a store with a partner. "Hudgins and Mitchem sat just around the corner on Gwynville Road," she said. Every neighborhood in Mathews County seemed to have several stores in the early twentieth century. One or more specialized in groceries and dry goods, another in farm equipment and fishing gear, another did wheelwright work and sold buggies and carriages. But they all seemed to have soft drinks in an icebox and later drink machines, and some tell of more than one general-merchandise store in the same neighborhood.

"Toody" enjoyed telling tales that her father and grandfather had told through the years. Like all the other stores in the county, her father's and grandfather's stores used nail kegs as stools for the people, who gathered to pass the time exchanging local news and gossip, to sit. They took eggs and chickens in exchange for commodities—there was a ready market for them in Baltimore. Often the customers received a due bill for later purchases. Little money circulated on the island back then.

While "Toody's" grandfather, was in business, a woman brought a hen in to trade for grocery items. She said, "This stubborn creature won't do anything but set--she's no good to me." Carney placed the hen in a separate coop with plans for her. After the customer left, he looked about for a suitable place to set the hen. Taking the keg that had been sitting upright for a trashcan, Carney filled it with straw, forming a nest in the center. Removing eggs from the crate he had filled for shipment, he placed them in the center. Carney fetched the hen that he had fed and watered, placing her in the nest. Some weeks later, a customer reported she heard chicks peeping under that hen on the nest when she entered the store. Carney felt well paid for his efforts when he ate fried chicken for supper a couple months later, knowing there would be more regularly in the next few weeks. But after the hen served his purpose, Carney shipped her in a crate with others.

Gwynn Post Office moved up Old Ferry Road near the churches at one time. (Back then, the Methodist Church held services in a church building that is now the Civic Center building. It sat on the opposite side of the road from its present location.) In my interviews, different dates were given for this location. All agreed one of the Godseys operated that store. Then the office operated from a small building that still sits near the present post office in later years. However, the spot the post office sits today has been its site through many of the years since it opened.

"Toody" told another story of by-gone days. Herbert Grimstead owned a store, with Gwynn Post Office in the corner, when Marge, a young-teen-age girl, had her first birthday party, inviting both boys and girls her age. Three of the boys invited had no way of making money to purchase a gift, and they knew their parents had none to give them. So they devised a plan to buy gifts for their friend. Finding an old fish box, the boys attached two strings to the corners of one end, placing some corn in the straw in front of the box. They hid in the barn loft at a neighbor's, where a good-size flock of fowl mingled. One held the two strings with the box sitting on end. When opportunity afforded itself, he lowered the box down over a rooster, by releasing the string so it fell face down on the ground. The other two boys ran from the barn to rescue their trophy.

Being as quiet as possible, they tied its legs and wings, tucking the bird under one boy's arm and heading for Grimstead's store. Two hid in the bushes, approaching the store, while the first boy went into the store. He explained to Mr. Grimstead that he needed a birthday present for a girl's party, but only had the rooster to buy it. So Grimstead suggested a box of stationery in even exchange, sending the boy to put the rooster in the chicken coop out back when he left the store.

Before too much longer, a second boy brought a rooster, wanting to exchange it for a girl's birthday gift. Grimstead said the only thing he had would be stationery. But he also explained someone else had already brought in a rooster very much like his and purchased that. The boy told him a girl could use two boxes of writing paper. Grimstead sent him out back to put the rooster into the coop when he left the store, telling him not to let the other fowl out.

Finally after a time, they could wait no longer so the third boy went in with the same rooster, it having never been in the coop. When Grimstead saw the teenager, he knew something was fishy. So the wise storekeeper let the boy relate the identical story the other two boys had told before suggesting they check the coop in the back of the store. Taking the boy and rooster out to the coop, it was just as Grimstead had guessed. The same rooster. Neither boy went to the party, but neither could either sit comfortably to eat his supper. "Toody" chuckled when she finished the tale that took place in her childhood.

Picture courtesy of John W. Dixon, who also did research as to the correct building, before taking photos.

Gwynn Post Office sat in the corner of this building, known as Godsey's Store, about 1915. It was either the second or third location of the office. The owner pays tribute with a sign over the front door. See pg 113 for another.

At the time of the hotel fire, Richard Godsey, known as "Dick", had a store on Old Ferry Road and the post office moved there with "Dick's" wife, Alice M. Godsey, as postmaster. Alice was a native of Baltimore and graduated from Peabody University—considered somebody special to the locals. The islanders enjoyed her piano playing as well as her service in the post office, where they learned what a delightful person she was. Alice retired after six years when her stepson, Robert N. Godsey, received an appointment for the job. Robert N. was known as "Nordey" by the island folk. However according to Gazelle Moore, Godsey never worked in the post office, but his sister, Ethel Godsey Deagle, acted as postmaster while he ran the store.

When Godsey retired from the post office in 1948, it moved to Herbert Grimstead's store. Ethel Deagle served as postmaster there until John Loop assumed his appointment in January 1948.

Gazelle Moore told of one postmaster after another, though not in the order of their service. She also commented that every store with a post office had a showcase of candy. The case sat on the counter so one had to ask the storekeeper for help with their purchase—it kept children's sticky fingers where they belonged. Like myself, she remembered the one-cent treats we had to enjoy when we arrived home.

I enjoyed an interview with Teeny Godsey Edwards, who lived on Gwynn's Island her lifetime. That is until she, as a widow unable to use her legs, felt she could no longer carry on alone in 2003. So Teeny moved to Mathews Convalescent Center. She and I had daughters in the same grade in high school, and I have decorated her house with draperies, dust ruffles and furniture covering several times during the time that I operated The Craftsman Shop. Still her friendly self, Teeny said when the store and post office burnt, Henry Grimstead owned the store that they were in. So he moved the post office immediately, putting it in the front downstairs bedroom on the first floor of his Victorian home. It sat across the road from the store. Accommodations for a separate entrance made it private, not interfering with their family's activities. As soon as the present building had been completed, it moved to the corner of the new store.

Postmasters continued to change every few years, but the post office has remained in the same building. In July

2001, Elizabeth Rowe received a transfer to Gwynn Post Office as postmaster and remains in service when I contacted her in 2004. "Liz," as her friends know her, reports 245 post office boxes with all rented. Gwynns Island has no home delivery with a Star Route carrier.

Grimstead Post Office

"The years teach us much the days never knew."
Ralph Waldo Emerson

Twelve more post offices opened in Mathews County after Gwynn, but before Grimstead. And sixteen years intervened between their openings, but it seems only fitting that it be considered before leaving Gwynn's Island. In fact, I had driven by Grimstead on Old Ferry Road, without noticing it was a post office.

The population of the entire United States increased during the last decades of the nineteenth century with flourishing economy after the states recovered from the Civil War. And Gwynn's Island was no exception. Many residents felt need of a second post office nearer the bustling activity at Callis Wharf. So after John B. Grimstead, who owned a store on the corners of Old Ferry Road and Callis Wharf Road, applied for one, he became postmaster in early February 1899.

Callis Wharf had a humble beginning during the Civil War when Captain William James Callis, known on the Island as "Captain Jim," traveled to Baltimore in a schooner. It had been the way to trade when boats were more common than land travel before automobiles. He carried products from the county and exchanged them for merchandise unavailable locally. On his return trips, Captain Jim backed up into the inlet and dumped the oyster shell ballast, slowly building a road under the waters near shore. He wanted a solid pier where he could dock his schooner. In time, he had built a wharf with oyster shells that has endured the worst of storms when others were totally destroyed.

It was about 1899 when the commercial steamers began to run from Baltimore to Callis Wharf and other wharfs in Mathews County. On the return trip they carried local products, replacing Captain Jim's need for making trips. In time his son, Walter Eugene Callis, made the dock larger, adding to the mound of oyster shells. He installed gas and oil service. By 1918, Elwood Eugene Callis, Sr. established a retail store at the site, and as it grew so did its popularity.

Callis Wharf had one of the largest seafood plants on the Eastern Coast of the United States in operation in the 1950's. Huge quantities of oysters and crabmeat were processed there—200 gallons of oysters a day and 5,500 pounds of crabmeat a week. Back then oyster season ran September through April. By the time the processing plant had a good cleaning, crabs would be ready to pick. (Facts from *History and Progress, Mathews County, Virginia,* published by MCHS)

Grimstead Post Office that had sufficient families to warrant the opening in its beginning, increased in the volume of mail through the years of progress at Callis Wharf and in the community. Leonard R. Callis, known as "Scrooch," worked at a store at the wharf and later joined John B. Grimstead as a partner in his store. Some years after the joint venture began, Grimstead retired from the post office. It was 1939 and "Scrooch" received an appointment to the position.

Janet E. Hurst became postmaster for two years in the mid-1940s. But during the same decade, J.R. Callis, Leonard's brother, joined "Scrooch" in the business. In time, there store burned so they built a new store with the post office in a smaller separate attached building on the left side. It had locked boxes that remain in use today. The brick store building on Old Ferry Road is where the Callis brothers built a business the entire county knew about, calling it

"Scrooch's Market." Some would drive from as far as New Point, at the opposite end of the county, to get a cut of their tender meat on the day it came in. Doris Loop worked as Callis's assistant postmaster, later accepting an appointment to the office. In my phone interview with Doris Loop, she said many customers called their meat orders in earlier, having him put their name on the package in the refrigerated area. Later the Callis brothers sold the business, but "Scrooch" resumed his position as postmaster again by 1946, serving until he retired in June 1970. Mrs. Loop assisted when he needed to be off. Then she served as Postmaster until March 1973. (Dates and statistics from research by Marguerite R. Sadler and Archives of the *Gloucester-Mathews Gazette-Journal*)

After Loop's retirement, OICs served until Betty-June Darden became official Postmaster in January 1989. Grimstead Post Office celebrated its 100th birthday on February 2, 1999 during Darden's service. Like all the centennials post offices celebrate, Darden served refreshments to all who attended the affair. Registration for a sheet of Civil War stamps brought interest with one lucky patron winning.

Each celebration brings memories of past days to older residents. When "Scrooch" Callis had the older store and served as postmaster, local boys enjoyed playing tricks on him. Once they climbed under the store building and bored a hole through the floor where they knew a bag of peanuts always sat. In fact, they bored far enough to puncture the bag, bringing a few peanuts out behind the large drill bit. The boys involved helped themselves on a regular basis. Wonder how long before Callis stopped the predators?

Darden retired May 2002 with OICs serving until Carol Jones received the appointment in August 2002. In our conversation, Jones reported that 148 of the 188 post office boxes are rented. There are no home deliveries.

Old Grimstead Store and Post Office 1937/38 with June Ladd, Alice Owens' roommate in college, and John Grimstead in the forefront (Mrs. Owens was very happy to have a part in the book when I contacted her about using the picture.)

North Post Office Established

"'Mamma,' complained little Elsie, 'I don't feel very well.' 'That's too bad, dear,' said mother sympathetically. 'Where do you feel worst?'' 'In school, Mamma.'" The Richardson Review *June 1927*

When North End Post Office closed in August 1866, residents at the northernmost end of Mathews County, at the gateway to Gloucester County, had to travel by horseback or horse and buggy to Mathews Court House to fetch their mail as they had done over half a century earlier. Eighteen years later, John W. Downs applied for another post office in a store building on John Clayton Highway.

The Civil War probably was a large reason for North End Post Office closing since the Union soldiers played havoc with most industry in the county. Every family had been affected before the war ended, when many of the rich had become poor. With all finances invested in shipyards, crops covering farmland, sawmills or slaves, they became a total lost with the destruction, and the slaves were freed.

The area of the county known as "North" today was known as "Battery" since long before Mathews became a county. *Mathews-Gloucester Gazette-Journal* published an article in March 1984, giving the history available about "Battery:"

"Milton Murray, II, of Mathews, said possible origins for the Battery name come from the large store of ammunitions Sir John Peyton of Isleham, North End's closest eastern neighbor in colonial times, bought during the Revolutionary war to help supply the local militia with arms. Murray also said that old records often have reference to the Kingston Parish battery. Kingston Parish had a chapel in its North River precinct."

Historians believe that the battery was located on the peninsula known today as Chapel Neck. Its boundaries are Blackwater Creek to the east, the North River to the south, Morgan's Branch or North End to the west and John Clayton Memorial Highway to the north. During the Civil War, their farms, milling businesses and boatyards were threatened by Union troops so they depended upon wit of the citizens. The four-story home on Blackwater Creek, formerly owned by Nancy Sweet, is named "Battery." During the war, it was used as a lookout post because the fourth story provided a detailed view of the surrounding fields and waterways.

Many local folk associate "Battery" that is defined by the dictionary as an emplacement for heavy guns with Fort Nonsense, the ruins of which are barely visible at the intersection of Windsor Road and John Clayton Memorial Highway today. However though the exact date of the fort's construction is unknown, the late W. Thomas Smith compiled a history of the structure in 1969. He revealed that conflicting sources say it was built during the Civil War to protect William Smart's important gristmill, or that it was simply fortified at that time and its actual construction was during the Revolutionary War. Whenever it was built, during the War Between the States, it proved to be useless as a defense of the mill. It appears its builders expected an attack from the Bay as the earthworks present a strong eastern front. However the Yankees attacked from the west and burned the mill. A. W. Soles is credited with giving the fort its name while viewing the remains after the battle and remarking, "My, what a piece of nonsense."

Although it may have been expected, Downs did not request "Battery" as the name for his post office, but he did request "North End." The National Archives show it as North Post Office, and so it was called when they approved Down (misspelling Downs) as the first postmaster on July 15, 1984. It is believed to have been in the corner of his hotel lobby. When the *Gloucester-Mathews Gazette- Journal* reporter did an interview with the late Estelle Smith in the 1984 article, she remembered a hotel with a dining room directly north of Chapel Neck Road. At that date, the building could still be seen, sitting back in the woods. The main customers were salesmen from Baltimore wholesale companies, and in later years also Norfolk companies, and travelers who were going or coming on the steamboat that used Auburn Wharf as one its docks. (Auburn Wharf was down Chapel Neck Road.) Downs served ten years as postmaster.

Henry Jones followed Downs as postmaster, but his store was located just a bit southeast of where North Post Office sits today. Folks who remember that site say Mrs. Jones took care of the mail as her husband's assistant. In little less than five years, it is believed to have moved again when Thomas F. Nelson became postmaster. He lived in the house now owned by Mrs. Thomas Edwards, called

"Elloree." Though we find no official record of the move, the late Mrs. Sands G. Jones remembered her mother-in-law saying the post office was in the corner of the Nelson yard at one time.

From whatever point Nelson operated the post office, he lost the position to Curtis A. Brown in November 1902, less than four years after accepting it. Brown owned a store that he had purchased from a Mr. Cawthorn. So he moved the post office into a corner of his building where it remained until he built a new store on his wife's family property, known as "Old Battery Farm." Curtis Brown remained postmaster until the month of his death in May 1939. His son, the late David Brown, told that his father worked from 6:00 a.m. until 11:00 p.m. six days a week until his last years when he closed "early'—6:30 or 7:00 p.m. When his father Curtis died, David Brown became postmaster and served until 1942.

At the time of Brown's retirement, North Post Office moved back across the highway to Sand Jones' store. His wife, Mary A. Jones, became postmaster. During the years that the Browns served in the post office, Henry Jones had built a new store on the site the post office now sits. Sands Jones joined his father, Henry, in business in the building in the 1920's, with Henry retiring in 1931. Mary A. Jones served as postmaster from July 1942 for 29 years until her retirement in September 1971.

William Gerald Jones, Sand's and Mary's son, who was assistant postmaster to his mother by then, was Officer in Charge for five months he told me in an interview. He received his official appointment in February of the following year. But it was 1962 when the father and son, partners by then, built the new brick building with a post office accessible from another entrance with locked boxes that patrons had access to day and night. The store continued to operate like that until the Sand Jones' death in 1975. Gerald and his wife, Joann, ran the store until July 1982 when he leased it to J. C. Brown Company, who converted it to a convenience store. Gerald remained postmaster until 2000 when he retired. In the years following, Bridgett Austin served as postmaster for a time. Today Officers in Charge see that the mail goes out and is placed in the proper boxes. Gerald Jones spoke of his time in the post office as pleasant years.

If you just visit this community, North Star Market serves delicious ice cream in cones or a plastic dish in whatever flavors you'd like. Others, who buy their lunch from the market, try to arrive before the freshly cooked chicken livers have sold out. Quite a different service from that offered in Mr. Downs' day.

I talked to the OIC in December 2004, learning North Post Office has 423 post office boxes of the 650 available rented. Highway carriers deliver to 231 families on two Star Routes, including the patrons they gained when Cardinal closed.

Bethel Community Gets Post Office

"Recent biographies of George Washington show that he was so much like the rest of us that we begin to feel sorry for him."
The Richardson Review, June 1927

The folks near Garden Creek and Winter Harbor, known as "Bethel"-- the name of the only church in the community since 1800, asked for a post office in late 1884. They had traveled long years to Port Haywood or Williams Wharf, fetching and posting their mail. With, Andrew Diggs' and Labin Hudgins' general merchandise store in the neighborhood on Route 611, Garden Creek Road, the four to ten mile trip became a bit bothersome. Hudgins obliged customers' pleas and applied for the post office. Who suggested the name, we don't know, but with Hudgins Post Office already in the county, the Post Office Department assigned Laban—spelt different than his name. It officially opened with Labin as postmaster on January 19, 1985. The post office served a large area before others opened. I have post cards in my files, dating near the opening date for the Brooks family, who lived over six miles from this new post office. The store was near Bethel United Methodist Church, and they lived in what today is Bashi Shores, adjoining the Bethel Beach area.

There were other postmasters through the years until George Anthony Hudgins and Wilbur C. Diggs purchased another store from Oscar Hudgins, then the post office moved a short distance down the road. Diggs became postmaster at the time, but the. Hudgins' son, Charlie D. Hudgins worked for his father. Diggs sold his half of the store to go to study for the ministry. And "Charlie Anthony" as the local folk knew him, accepted his appointment as postmaster on March 6, 1914. According to an interview with by a *Glo-Quips'* newspaper reporter in 1975, the store was located across from the small building Laban Post Office occupied in its later years. "Charlie Anthony" Hudgins operated the store and post office until he retired from the post office in 1951.

When Hudgins closed the post office, his assistant, Martha Helen Diggs, became postmaster, moving into a new small building. The office had to be closed seven weeks during this transition. Helen continued as postmaster of Laban Post Office after she married Emmett Lilly and worked until the Post Office Department closed this office in 1974.

The small building was sold to a local businessman to be used for his children's playhouse.

Courtesy Mary Campbell Diggs, who resides in Virginia Beach and has a small home in Mathews County

Helen Diggs Lilly in front of the building in which she was the first and last to serve as postmaster of Laban Post Office

Moving post offices

"Destiny is not a matter of chance, it's a matter of choice. It is not a thing to be waited for, it is a thing to be achieved."
William Jennings Bryant

Most every post office that stayed open moved through the years with some relocating many times. Today moving a post office is quite a task with locked boxes, most open to the actual work area on the back side, remaining mail for patrons, records, multiple forms, cash registers, scales, charge machines and computers, depending on the size of the post office. Instead of one stamp for the particular post office, their are many others from "Registered" to "Fragile." But before locked boxes, moving the post office could to be completed in short order. The cage, with bars within a window, surrounded by a frame, containing pigeonhole spaces on the backside, provided the new postmaster a safe place to store the mail. Postmasters became responsible for their own cages. The one post office stamp with the inkpad, the few forms used in that day, scales, and any remaining mail made the move quickly. There were no computers—just a cash box and later a cash register in the larger offices.

Picture courtesy *Mathews-Gloucester Gazette-Journal* 1993

The inside of a post office cage that has been reversed in the last days Bavon Post Office served the community. Either the last name of each family or all with the same initials fill each bin. June Brown is attending the mail.

Changes in Mail Service

"A small girl asked her mother: 'If I grow up will I have a husband like papa?' 'Yes, my dear,' mother replied. 'And if I do not get married will I be an old maid like Aunt Susan?' 'Yes, you will,' was the reply. The little girl thought for a moment, put her hands to her head and said, "Well, I am in a fix."' The Richardson Review June 1927

In a recent conversation with Dana Brown, Postmaster at Mathews, I mentioned that today she only had to cancel outgoing mail. And little of the outgoing mail is cancelled until it reaches the central post office with new machines for automatic canceling in Richmond, Virginia. It is a contrast to the early days when both outgoing and incoming mail were both canceled by hand. She said, "We'd never get the mail completed if it had to be stamped when it came in." At two o'clock in the afternoon, two of her clerks continued to place morning mail in the individual boxes. Meanwhile, Brown helped customers with outgoing mail, stamping it before she placed it in the outgoing trays. Another truck would arrive at four o'clock with more mail. That isn't mentioning mail, which had been prepared in the proper pick-up area for Highway Carrier delivery. Thankfully, it comes from Richmond in the proper bins.

Backs and feet tire with the constant preparation of outgoing mail plus two truckloads a day to sort. I questioned Brown about Mathews Post Office today. There are 1,141 post office rented boxes and 210 families, who receive mail by highway carriers on Star Routes from Mathews Post Office. But the three mail trucks, leaving this, the central distribution point, also deliver to 15 other post offices and a total of 1,200 mailboxes on the highways of the county.

Now with technology and automation, Richmond Post Office uses machines to separate the mails for each post office. It comes to the Mathews Post office in tubs, ready for the three truck drivers to load. All items mailed in Mathews to other post offices in the county or elsewhere, go to Richmond—our distribution center, where it will be stamped if it hasn't been. Hopefully, the letter will return on the truck the following day.

Through the years the county had a total of 44 post offices—though that many were never operating at one time. In December 1910, there were 35 post offices, operating in Mathews County. However, more mail came directly to the many wharves than by land. In that case, it need not go farther except the mail addressed to Mathews Post Office or another one nearby. By 1934, all the wharves had closed with the mail transferred to the nearest post office. Trucks and buses brought mail into Mathews County, and the post offices had increased to 38. Drop offs were made along the way, but many of the bags came directly to Mathews Post Office. Though that was not near the volume they have today for the one office.

The county's population has grown, leaving fewer acres for farming. Some areas have actually become sub divisions where cotton, tobacco, wheat, corn or hay grew earlier. Catalogs have increased the post office's volume of mail, for which they delight because it brings in more revenue. When a catalog is used, parcel post arrives, enabling more profit for the post office. Since I wear a woman's petite, I am a constant user of catalogs, few stores carrying my size. But sometimes the sizes vary so I pay more postage to return the item. Many medications, both prescription drugs and non-prescription vitamins, supplements and herbs come by mail.

With one or two post offices closing each year, I asked Brown what determined the closings. She readily answered, "Safety and lack of a proper building." Since I began the research for this book, I constantly have people say to me, "I don't want my post office to close. I enjoy the break in the day to pick up mail and chat." These are not all retired people, but many are self-employed or work locally.

Chapter Five

Community Requested Blakes Post office

"That confiding in the integrity, ability, and punctuality of the said James T. Brooks I do commission him a Postmaster, authorized to perform the duties of that Office at Blakes aforesaid, according to the laws of the United States and the Regulations of the Post Office Department: To hold the said office of Postmaster with all the powers, privileges, and emoluments there unto belonging, during the pleasure of the Postmaster General of the United States." (Post Office Appointment of third postmaster of Blakes, dated 1st day of February 1907.)

A general store, blacksmith shop and other businesses congregated in a small community 2 ½ miles south of Cobbs Creek Post Office and 3 ½ miles north of Hudgins Post Office when Grover Cleveland was president. Tired of hearing about and having to travel a distance for mail, Robert H. Blake applied to the First Assistant Postmaster General, A. E. Stevensen, on August 12, 1886 for a post office to service the 2,150 people in the vicinity according to his application. Since Mathews County residents had no rural delivery, more post offices became a necessity with new communities. The post office would sit on Route 11183, now Route 198 or Buckley Hall Road. Blake made it clear that the mail truck passed the proposed stop six days a week. The village, with several homes besides the businesses, around the post office became known as "Blakeville," according to what Dorothy D. White's mother-in-law had told her when she moved to the community. However, Mary Foster Brooks, a lifetime resident, says she knew it as "Blaketown."

The official post office application required the names of the nearest river, creek and the nearest railroad.

Piankitank was the nearest river, one mile south of the location, and Chapel, the nearest creek one half mile southeast. Blake named Richmond (the city was 100 miles away before the Highway Department leveled the roads through New Kent County, where one felt like he was riding a roller coaster) and York River as the nearest railroads. The application required a diagram of the location on a grilled section of the second page.

Robert H. Blake became postmaster of the post office, bearing his name on October 11. 1886. He continued in the position for 11 years until August 1897. At that time Robert T. Brooks succeeded him, serving almost 10 years. Lavalle Wilson furnished me with a copy of the appointment of her grandfather, James T. Brooks, as Postmaster at Blakes on February 1, 1907. The document from the Post Office Department bears the signature of F. H. Hitchcock, Acting Postmaster General.

The population of 2,150 residents dwindled as the Postmaster General approved other post offices in the neighborhoods farthest from Blakes Post Office. Merchants had established general merchandise stores when they saw the need. Then the customers called for a post office with a well-stocked store for their other necessities.

By 1916, Henry Foster had opened his blacksmith business and became a licensed undertaker in 1926 according to his daughter-in-law, Marjorie B. Foster. Ten years later her husband, Wilbert, received his license. Later Marjorie passed the exam, becoming the third undertaker in the family. After automobiles replaced carriages and buggies with fewer farmers using horse-drawn machinery, the blacksmith shop closed. Both Henry and Wilbert Foster put full time in the funeral home business. Realizing need for a sizable chapel and a more central location, they built and moved to a new facility at Mathews Court House in 1954. However, Foster Funeral Home had really put Blakes on the map for residents living in other parts of the county.

After James Brooks retired as postmaster in 1940, women filled the position of postmaster until the office closed on May 15, 1987. Many still remember these postmasters: Naomi Thompson, Virginia German, Ernestine Haynes and Dana Brown, who is now postmaster at Mathews Post Office.

In 1987 the post office occupied a building owned by the Church of God, whose chapel sat across the road in the former Foster Funeral Home building. When the lease expired, the church requested it be terminated, as allowed by contract at their option, on May 15, 1987 according to a *Gloucester-Mathews Gazette-Journal* report. This provided opportunity for the United Postal Service to close the small post office, sending all mail to Cobbs Creek P. O. Field Division Manager/Postmaster Neil Perkins had already informed the county administrator, Frank Pleva, and the Mathews Board of Supervisors of plans to consolidate the two post offices, using a larger facility earlier in 1986. However renovations of the larger location in Richard Callis's offices had not been completed when the lease expired.

The situation put an added burden on the Cobbs Creek Postmaster, Colanne Bunting, who already had only 260 boxes for the 300 families and businesses in Cobbs Creek—an increase from 65 boxes needed in 1983. The post office moved across Buckley Hall Road to the larger location with sufficient boxes for all patrons on June 1, 1987.

Jean Davis was Officer in Charge at Blakes before the post office closed. She presented a petition, signed by the residents, asking that Blakes Post Office remain. "The petition cited the inconvenience of informing correspondents of change of address and added distance to travel for mail service as reasons for objection to the consolidation." (*Gloucester-Mathews Gazette-Journal* July 3, 1986) Evidence proves it was denied.

Residents of Blakes regretted such a closing though the improved highway had shortened the distance to Cobbs Creek Post Office to one mile. Today most patrons in Blakes receive Highway Carrier delivery on the Star Route. But to purchase stamps, mail packages or buy money orders, it means a trip up the road to the post office. For Dorothy White, who is legally blind and hasn't been able to drive a car since 1990, it means finding someone to drive her since she lost her husband. Her surviving daughter lives in Suffolk, Virginia.

"The Comforter"

"Anxious Old Lady—I say, my good man, is this boat going up, or down? Deck Hand—Well, she's a leaky old tub, mum, so I shouldn't wonder if she was going down. But then, again, her b'ilers ain't none too good, so she might go up."
Chicago Leader September 1911

Picture courtesy the Gloucester-Mathews *Gazette-Journal*

Blakes Post Office in its last home. See pg. 113.

Bohannon the eighteenth Post Office

"If you haven't got anything nice to say about anybody, come sit next to me." Alice Roosevelt Longworth

Hicks Wharf Post Office sat a distance off East River Road with a sizeable community, having formed on roads branching to the right and left. However, a community had formed farther to the south on East River Road. Mr. Cyrus White operated a store in 1887 in this neighborhood where many families lived on smaller farms, amounting to about 400 people. They had two general stores, a boarding house, a tide mill, a one-room schoolhouse and an oyster shucking business. Yet they had to travel too many miles to Hicks Wharf or North to send or obtain any mail. This was reason enough for William F. Davis to apply for a post office to be located in the corner of Mr. White's general merchandise store. The *Gloucester-Mathews Gazette- Journal* archives show that he requested the new office be called "White's Neck Post Office."

Davis first request was denied so he suggested "Bohannon" as a substitute. Today the residents give two reasons why the name was chosen. First, some feel it was for a "drummer" (slang for a traveling salesman of the late 1800's), named Bohannon. He stayed in the boarding house across the road from White's Store, making friends with the customers on his frequent trips. Second, a Bohannon family owned a larger plantation on North River Road. Thus what better name than using the name for their new post office?

Davis received his official appointment on November 28, 1887 as the postmaster and served 15 years. Onie A White, who fell heir to his father's business, obtained the position following Davis, serving for 20 years. Politics didn't seem to effect the postmaster's position in some post offices while in others, the postmaster shifted with changes of the party, governing in our national capitol. Linda Steger served eight years before Frances White became postmaster in

December 1930. The National Archives record they changed her name to Frances D. Anderton May 8, 1935. However, she kept the position until 1980, having served 50 years as postmaster. But during her time of service, the post office moved from White's Store to its own small building where it sits today. When Mrs. Anderton retired, her son, Charles Ralph, became postmaster. Known in the community as Ralph Anderton, he held the position until October 2003. Officers in Charge have served since. One resident said the post office was referred to as "the building with three light bulbs" while Ralph served the post office. When I faced him with the description, he replied, "The women folks have dressed up the building since they've been serving."

Picture courtesy Ralph Anderton

Otis A. White on his store porch about 1910. Bohannon Post Office sat in the corner where White served as postmaster from 1902 to 1922. Snow still lay on the porch.

Lorraine Roane, a lifetime resident in the community, told a *Gloucester-Mathews Gazette-Journal* reporter in 1989 that Dr. C. M. Rains, who had an office on Rains' Lane, cared for the sick of the community. He was remembered as a very caring person, who traveled with a patient to Norfolk on the steamer when one required hospitalization. In fact, Mrs. Roane believed that Dr. Rains had planned to open a hospital on his lane, but it never materialized.

Since the post office located on East River Road sat near "the turnpike," connecting that road with North River Road, it drew more patrons. "Old timers" described Turnpike Road as little more than a mud puddle in the early years according to Roane. Rob Roy Roane, Lorraine's husband, moved from Gloucester County to Bohannon when they wed. He enjoyed visiting one of the stores in the evenings to hear the "old timers" tell tales of past years. They had attended the one-room schoolhouse at the end of Mill Road. That road led to L.K. West's tide mill and an oyster-shucking house.

Residents in the early twentieth century attended Peninsula School, where they not only learned in school, but also enjoyed the same type social life as described in other communities with plays, socials and May Days. Audrey Mae Mason kindly provided information regarding the school and use of the building since it closed. She said that Paul Hobday initiated the original high school in 1905 when there were elementary schools in each community in Whites Neck. In time Mobjack, Bohannon and the other elementary schools closed, with all the children attending Peninsula School. In 1939, Mathews High School became home to all high school students in Mathews County. However, Peninsula School continued to teach elementary classes until it closed its doors in 1946. Then all the children climbed on buses, attending consolidated schools in Mathews, leaving earlier and returning later.

Mason said George Philpotts purchased the school building from the county. Further research showed Philpotts sold the property to Odd Fellows Lodge No. 273 in 1950. Members not only used it for their meetings, but the County used it as a polling place. The Lodge also made its facilities available for community use, and members provided parties, socials, entertainment and sporting events for community participation. In 1987 the West Mathews Community League organized. About 1989, the League purchased the former Peninsula School building from the Odd Fellows Lodge. Mason said that the League holds both luncheon meetings in winter and evening meetings during summer months. Three fundraisers each year contributes to maintenance: A fair in the spring, a chicken barbeque in the summer and a spaghetti supper in winter. With the money raised in these affairs and small grants, the League has been able to keep the building in repair with an attractive lawn.

Today, the bustling business community has little more than the post office, one general store, a firehouse and its residents with years of exciting history. The post office has a friendly atmosphere where neighbor meets neighbor. Beverly Gayle grew up in the community, having returned in recent years, and assisted in the post office when I talked to her in 2004. She enjoys contact with the natives and welcomes the new residents. In our conversation about Bohannon Post Office, where she substituted, I learned about events and those serving today. The weekend of Memorial Day 2004, Jean Hall, the OIC, celebrated with the many veteran patrons. Throughout the day on Friday May 28th, she displayed a scrapbook with pictures and commentaries of veterans from the community. It contained items from the Civil War, continuing to recent conflicts. She offered door prizes with three winners. When they drew for the American Flag, Earl Havenner's name was pulled. Earl, a Vietnam and Desert Storm Veteran, was dying of cancer. He wanted this flag placed on his casket instead of the government issued one. With this much caring by the ones serving the small community, they don't want a change.

The small post office still only offers General Delivery with 60 pigeonholes, each for a sir name. More than one family will be found in most of the pockets. Forty-four families receive highway carrier service on Bohannon's Star Route.

Foster Post Office Established

"The height of Foolishness is to discard an opportunity without full and proper investigation."
Benjamin Franklin

By 1892, another hamlet had come together near John Clayton Memorial Highway, south of North Post Office and near the head of East River, known as "Tick Neck".

I contacted 91-year-old Estelle Ashberry West, who lives in Gloucester, Virginia. She was born and raised in "Tick Neck," where houses dotted the road at intervals, leading to the water and the shoreline. According to her, there was a general merchandise store on the left side of East River Road, near the corner of John Clayton Memorial Highway and a two-room schoolhouse just beyond that. Less than a quarter mile farther down the road, a blacksmith shop operated. A church sat on the right side a distance farther south.

When "Foster" School opened, the *Mathews Journal* announced the occasion in a September 1914 issue: "Foster school has opened with a full attendance, with Eunice Soles as principal and Miss Bessie Major as assistant." The two-room school housed grades one through seven, and West reminded me that the building is a residence today.

Members of First Baptist Church, Hudgins, who lived in the hamlet, organized a church in a home by 1886, according to *History and Progress of Mathews County, Virginia,* published by MCHS. They built Macedonia Baptist Church in1887 for the approximate cost of $100. An oil burner explosion caused extensive damage to the sanctuary in December 1951. They repaired the damage in August 1952 to its present condition at the cost of $2,700. The church still has regular services with two or more additions, having been made to the original structure. The $100 chapel has grown to a church, costing many thousands.

The residents and businessmen thought it time they stop traveling up the road to North Post Office for mail by late 1891. Since the mail truck passed by the store six days a week, why couldn't they have a post office? So it took little persuasion for William T. Foster to apply for one. He requested the name "Watchwand," and then "Church Branch." Both were denied. Hence the Post Office Department honored Mr. Foster by naming it for him, making it official in February 1892. The office sat in the corner of another Mr. White's general merchandise store. William E. Iverson and John W. Everage were appointed as postmasters in the earlier months of 1901, but both declined appointment according to the National Archives. In September of that year, Lorenzo E. Atherton accepted the position, moving the office to his store around the corner on Route 14, John Clayton Memorial Highway. He served 12 years.

The blacksmith shop closed when demand for the work had vanished. They closed the school and sold the building. Children had been sent by bus to larger county schools. Atherton's store burnt in the early 1920s. Thus the post office moved across the road to the general merchandise store that Walter M. Shawn operated. Shawn became postmaster in December 1924. Interviewing John Edward Ashberry, a native of "Tick Neck," he remembered Shawn well from his boyhood days. Mary Cannon Godsey, formerly of Mathews, offered Shawn's picture for the book. However, except where postmasters' pictures from the past include the post office, I'm eliminating the same. Shawn served until the end of January 1940.

Morris Curfman, with his wife Mae, used a house near Shawn's general merchandise store for bottling sodas of various kinds, increasing interest in the neighborhood. According to West, for a time, while the business grew, the Curfmans lived in an upstairs apartment over the business with their son Jimmy. Later, they built a modern ranch style home next to the business.

L. E. Murphy purchased the store building after some years. His wife, Katherine A. Murphy, received her appointment as postmaster of Foster Post Office in 1973, but had to lay her duties aside by 1977 due to illness. An OIC took care of the post office. It was during her illness that Murphy built a separate 300 square foot building to house the post office. It moved into the new building in 1980 with Mary Ann Smith the new postmaster. (Many of the facts about Foster P.O. were published in the *Gloucester-Mathews Gazette-Journal* March 21, 1985.)

Virginia Ann Shipley became the postmaster in March 1983. The post office moved from the 300 square foot building, which had become too small with the growing population, to the empty store building, having been remodeled for the post office, in 1986. It was a more difficult move than earlier ones had been with 95 boxes to relocate, plus moving all other equipment. It remains at the site in 2004. When I talked to Shipley, she said there has been one increase after another in volume. In June 2004, she reported 143 boxes with 92 rented and 89 Star Route families with home delivery.

Mobjack Post Office Located in White's Neck

"Does thou love life? Then do not squander time,
for that's the stuff life is made of."
Benjamin Franklin

The name all began with the Indians, calling the point where East River empties into a bay, by a name meaning "bad land." Thus white men derived "Mock." According to tradition, a pirate named "Jack" was mobbed and thrown overboard in the Bay near this point. The name Mockjack dates back to as early as 1652 when the General Assembly referred to it. In records after 1800, the name changes to "Mobjack." Sounds like it all came from the mobbing of a pirate, doesn't it? The name referred to the small bay, extending from New Point Comfort to Guinea in Gloucester County. (Facts from Charles E. Hatch's book *Mathews County Places & Names, p. 71,* in MCHS archives.)

The land owned by the Whites, Armisteads, who intermarried with the Gwynns of Gwynn's Island, and Gayles, among others, made up this neck. Cyrus White, one of the early landowners, purchased 40 acres from Arthur B. White of York County for the sum of $325 in 1850. The place was referred to as Mill Point and "40 acres adjoining lands of Elizabeth Armistead and others estimated to contain 41 acres of land belonging to the same tract of land belonging to the estate of Francis Armistead." (Quote from Deed Book II in Mathews Clerk's Office)

It is evident that the Armisteads owned "Myrtle Grove," now owned by Wilson and Turner Davis. Their grandfather, Wilson Davis bought 70 acres, including the farmhouse from Anna Marie Gwynn in 1890. According to the deed the land was previously owned by Mrs. Elizabeth Armistead, wife of Francis Armistead." (Archives of the *Gloucester-Mathews Gazette-Journal)*

In 1871 Caleb S. Maltby transferred the title of a deed to Hezekiah T. Philpotts in Deed Book II in Mathews County Clerk's Office records. The land sat at the end of the neck where the East River and Mobjack Bay meet. H. T. Philpotts, known as Captain Thornton, divided the land into 31 lots to sell.

John F. Philpotts, Captain Thornton's nephew, saw need for a post office by 1892 since the population had reached 200. He applied and became the first postmaster in September. The National Archives states: "'Windmill Point' requested for the name, but denied, 'too long.'" He reported that Bohannon was the nearest post office to Mobjack. The office to be located in the corner of Oscar Nelson Walker's general store became officially Mobjack Post Office, opening in September 1892 with John Philpotts as postmaster.

Next to Walker's general store, Mr. O. Rhea had a dry goods store, and Dr. James operated a drug store next to that. They all sat on the waterfront.

Captain Thornton Philpotts began selling lots in 1897. A farmer, land developer and builder of Philpotts Wharf, he recognized need for a place to worship in the community. Thus he set aside a piece of land for a Methodist Church. In 1898, Grace Methodist, with opened doors, welcomed the residents. "Every home was represented in the church," Sally Bett Walker Lawson had commented. Today, the church is known as Grace-Providence United Methodist Church. Additions have been added to the original sanctuary, where a congregation continues to meet.

The Senior Philpotts deeded four lots, measuring 30' x 105' each, one joining the other to his son George in 1906. The deed said the streets carried the names Grace and Pearl Streets. It was George, who built the Philpotts "business district" from the waterfront land and a larger wharf. Much of the land near the waterfront, being very low, George had built with oyster shells, according to his daughter, Mary Philpotts Hudgins.

The gift deed to George had conditions attached to it. Referring to his son, George, as the 'party of the second part," Philpotts instructed: " second part shall not sell, or traffic in any way, any kind of intoxicating liquors, nor would he or anyone who may hereafter own said land." The second condition read: "Said land shall not be sold to anyone of African extraction or it shall revert back to H. T. Philpotts and his heirs." (Deed Book II Mathews' Clerk's Office)

The Walker General Store furnished room for a post office and carried "everything a store could hold," according to his granddaughter, Sally Bett Walker Lawson. From her childhood she remembered candies, at least 12 varieties of cookies and her grandmother's homemade ice cream that the store carried. A 1916 ledger reveals some prices of the day: A box of cornflakes for ten cents, five pounds of lard cost 85 cents, two pounds sausage 30 cents, Ivory® soap five cents a bar, and 16 yards of cotton materials cost $1.60. (*Gloucester-Mathews Gazette-Journal* archives credited with most of the above information.)

By the early 1900's deliveries no longer depended on the slow sloops, but steamboats delivered and picked up daily except Sundays. Life changed at Philpotts Wharf when the steamer Mobjack, a side-wheeler, appeared on the scene. Mail and, in hot weather, ice were the certain items every day. Fifty-gallon drums of fuel oil made up part of the deliveries—a bit dangerous for a steamer with passengers. If the boiler blew, it would be an even worse explosion and destruction. Crash! Thump! Bang!

Special orders from Norfolk Companies came overnight when ordered by telephone. Though few homes had telephones, businesses had them as soon as lines came into the county. One called central from the wooden box attached to the wall. Central dialed the person or operator in a city that you needed to reach. Every phone was on a party line with so many long and so many short rings, designating your phone until the 1940's. In fact, my husband Kirby and I began operating "The Craftsman Shop" without access to a phone line. When we finally acquired a line and phone service, we were on a party line until we moved the business from our home site to Mathews Court House in 1963.

The steamer Mobjack never left empty, but crates of eggs and chickens helped add to the freight. All types of seafood left on this steamer. When in season, fresh fish had to be iced down in a special bin when shipped. Philpotts Wharf was just one of her stops so she didn't carry a full load from the one stop.

The steamer left Norfolk early in the morning, stopped at all East River Wharfs (Diggs, Williams, Hicks and Philpotts) every day; at Severn and North River Wharfs on Monday, Wednesday and Friday; at Ware River wharfs on Tuesday and Thursday. So it was late afternoon when it arrived back in Norfolk.

Passengers had to board at the wharf nearest to them and return the same route. My grandmother Callis and my daddy, her youngest son, made about two trips a year to Norfolk. She went to shop, but spent the nights with relatives. They left Williams Wharf in early afternoon, arriving in Norfolk later, spending the night. The next day they traveled from her cousins to town by streetcar, returning the same way. The third day they traveled on the Mobjack back to Mathews. She died when daddy was ten years old, but the trips left vivid memories that he related many times to my sister and me. In fact, in 1933 during the Great Depression, Daddy went back to sea for some months. Momma and we girls visited relatives in Norfolk and Hampton during that summer. While at her Aunt's home in Berkley section of Norfolk, Daddy showed us his cousin's house where he had spent those nights with treasured memories. From the late 1800s until the first decade of the twentieth century, Berkley was an elite section of Norfolk.

Fares would be hard to calculate on today's computers. The boat fare was $1 plus ten cents for the wharf fee at Williams Wharf, costing $1.10 each way. Meals were fifty cents each for "a fine meal"—dinner soon after midday instead of lunch. If Norfolk residents wanted an inexpensive outing, they could board the Mobjack at 6:30 a.m., ride all day; buy their meal, and return in the afternoon, all for $1.50 each. There was only one obstacle, if anyone got off at a wharf in Gloucester or Mathews, they had to pay 10 cents both to come ashore and to board—a total of 20 cents each at each port—wharfage fee. Freight fees were even worse to calculate. There was a different charge for each item: two cents for a crate of eggs, five cents for a barrel of flour and eight cents for a barrel of sugar were standard rates for either picking up or discharging. The fees were figured in the total freight bill. At the end of a given period, the fright line remitted a check to the wharf operator, including charges collected for passengers and freight.

Robert Morton Sigman, who was purser on Steamer Mobjack, revealed in *History and Progress of Mathews County, Virginia*, published by MCHS, that the captain did more than work for the Steamboat Company. "'In summer,' Mr. Sigman remembers, 'we carried large amounts of ice. This was a particular privilege of the captain. He bought the ice in Old Point and sold it in Gloucester and Mathews Counties at the wharfs. I think he probably made more out of selling ice than he did out of his salary." He continued to tell how the ice melted down one quarter or one third on a hot day.

Older residents, who either remember or had parents or grandparents that relived the events often in conversation, relate interesting tales concerning activities when the Mobjack arrived at Philpotts' Wharf. Many met the steamboat Mobjack daily, knowing it would arrive at 10:30 in the morning. They'd drive their horse and buggy to the rail fence around the shore where they tied the horse. If women came, they dressed properly. They had combed their hair and wore a proper dress, probably made of cotton, or a blouse and skirt. In the early days, their polished shoes were buttoned to the top. They called this area of Mobjack "down to the front." (Information from *Gloucester-Mathews Gazette-Journal* archives)

I talked to Wilson Davis, who carries his grandfather's name. He was born, grew up and still lives at "Myrtle Grove." His grandfather related that as soon as the captain or porter brought the mailbag into the store, a resident dumped the contents in the middle of the floor. Each man grabbed anything with his name on it, passing the other pieces to the neighbors, saying, "I have a letter," or "this is yours." What a scramble! The postmaster had few to stamp and hold when they finished sorting. In those days, mail was stamped at point of departure, and post offices placed a second stamp when it arrived. I feel by the time the Post Office Inspectors reached Mobjack, the practice didn't last too long.

Since Captain Thornton divided the lots equally before he sold them, neighbor could talk to neighbor over the yard fence every day. It became a close-knit community. In the 1980s, Walker's granddaughter, having left and lived in cities, spoke of her hometown as "a pretty little village" that was like a "big family."

The Philpotts' family not only sold lots for homes, they provided jobs. George operated an oyster shucking business in winter. In spring, the business continued to operate, but workers picked crabs. Work on the wharf kept responsible laborers busy six days a week. Offices to serve the many businesses hired secretaries and bookkeepers—the same person usually did both jobs and by hand.

While Philpotts' Wharf kept busy with the oil and gasoline distribution, first by steamboat and then by truck, so did the Davis's at "Myrtle Grove." They unloaded other freighters, carrying fertilizer from Norfolk and coal from Baltimore on boats, delivering just those items on a wharf across the creek from Philpotts' wharf. The freighters left with potatoes, watermelons, sweet corn, cantaloupes and whatever else might be in season.

When the unnamed hurricane hit in 1933, it destroyed much of Philpotts wharf and damaged buildings on the waterfront extensively. The businesses closed and buildings deteriated to the point of danger. In 1991, the families across the road from them cleared the debris, enjoying the view of Mobjack Bay from their front porches for the first time.

In 1934, E.L.H. Machen founded Mobjack Nurseries up East River Road from the waterfront. John Lee Machen managed the business when his father retired, seeing it grow by leaps and bounds. John Lee, Jr. has joined the linage of managers. The family continues to operate the business in the twenty-first century though most of their laborers come from places beyond Mobjack. Machen families enjoy living on the water though the business is a few streets back of them. In fact, John Lee, Jr. and his wife, Cindy, live in the last building that housed the post office. (Information gathered in an interview with Pam Machen and *Gloucester-Mathews Gazette-Journal* archives.)

Mobjack Post Office moved from Walker's general store to Anderton's general store on the opposite corner of Grace Street from the church. In later years, it had its own building on Grace Street. September 1960 when Dwight D. Eisenhower was president, Mary C. Haislep became postmaster, serving until the end of September 1992—a total of 32 years. Haislep followed a long line of family tradition. Her grandfather had served as postmaster of Mobjack for five years. And her mother, Linda Lewis Steger, was postmaster at both Bohannon and Foster. Haislep had been her mother's leave replacement officer at Foster Post Office the last five years that her mother served as postmaster. So when she applied for postmaster at Mobjack, she knew the work.

Haislip liked people, making the job enjoyable the 12 years she served in her neighborhood. She told a *Gloucester-Mathews Gazette-Journal* reporter at the time of her retirement, "You have to be a real people person for this job." She went on to explain that it helped to know people personally and to know their interests. The difficulty of distributing mail had increased before box numbers because there were so many people in Mobjack with the same name. It was because of the large amount of Whites living at this address that it had been called "White's Neck." Many had the same initials or even names. If she knew the interests of the occupants of a household, she'd be sure to give them magazines and catalogs accordingly.

The Post Office Department encouraged Haislip to take retirement a year early since they needed to downgrade post offices in the county. The office served 260 people, 60 more than when it opened in 1892. All mail goes through Fosters Post Office and is delivered by Highway Carrier. Norma Haislip remembered the days she spent with her mother in the post office fondly both in a letter and my interview.

For long years, my Granddaddy and Granny Richardson traveled to Mathews County from first Norfolk, then Newport News and lastly Hampton, every weekend, rotating their stays with first mother's sister and then our home. In 1931, Granddaddy had read about a bustling business district not yet affected by the depression. So on a Sunday afternoon, he wanted our family to join him, visiting Mobjack. We four piled into Granddaddy's car with my grandparents, driving to this place of which I'd never heard. For my sister and me, going from Fitchetts to Mobjack in that day, was equivalent to traveling the 90 miles to Richmond today. We only had a horse and wagon. I usually fussed under my breath in the automobile because I had to sit on the front seat between Daddy and Granddaddy, who didn't talk about things of interest to me. But not this time because I wanted to see. When they said, "Here it is," Granddaddy drove very slowly. I felt I was looking at a magazine picture. A white church with a steeple sat on the corner with white houses lining the streets and painted store buildings across the road on the water. Fitchetts seemed to get darker brown each year so this was a contrast for me at age five. A second row of houses sat back of the ones near the front on the Bay. It didn't matter that everything was closed because I could see more without people mulling around. I took a mental picture, dreaming about the church with a steeple and white houses with mown lawns at night. But I couldn't remember the funny name—"Mobjack." Actually it was many years later when working in a home opposite the church that I realized that was the street I had dreamed about in my childhood. The business buildings were no longer painted, but falling down from the many hurricanes after the one in 1933, which had closed them.

Picture courtesy the *Mathews-Gloucester Gazette-Journal*

Anderton's Store where Mobjack Post Office moved after 1933 Hurricane

A building that housed Gwynn Post Office after Godsey's store.

An end view of the general merchandise store that housed Blakes Post Office for many years.

Chapter Six

Dixie Post Office Opens near the Piankitank

The man whose inquiring nature asks 'how' goes farther than he who asks 'why.'" The Richardson Review, July-August 1927

The Colonial Estate named "Providence" sat high on a hill overlooking the Piankitank River in the upper west side of Mathews County, and the entire estate included surrounding lands. Mr. Fitchett had built the brick three-story mansion about 1750. An eminent English botanist laid out the garden according to Emmie Ferguson Farrar in her book, *Old Virginia Houses Vol. I.*

The Howlett family purchased the estate in 1799, renaming it "Howlett Hall." *The Mathews-Gloucester Gazette-Journal* reported after their research in April 1983 that it's believed the Howletts built the dock. Mr. Howlett, a descendent of the original owner, served as wharf agent for the steamers as owners of other large plantations did, according to his daughter, Elizabeth Howlett Sibley. She also said, "In those days, schooners brought wares to sell at the wharves in the county." The steamboats brought shipments from Baltimore, and in turn they left with lumber, cotton, tobacco, grain and seafood.

Along with the other shipments on the boats, a stash of mail came on each trip. A document in the National Archives states that mail was delivered to Green Point on a steamer from Baltimore twice a week. Sibley believes her father kept it stored in a special location in the warehouse and distributed the mail as residents came to the wharf, most often meeting the steamer.

So by 1893, when Grover Cleveland had been elected president, Charley C. Blake, a carpenter and builder of boats, saw need for an official post office. On his application, he made note of mail already being delivered to Green Point Wharf by the steamer from Baltimore. What better name than "Dixie" since Howlett Hall looked like fine plantation houses in the Deep South? Regarding the Dixie Post Office's first location, most believed it sat in a building just east of the steamboat wharf on the estate of Howlett Hall. Blake accepted the appointment to become the first postmaster in April 1893.

Just 18 months later, Lucy Howlett became the new postmaster, operating from the plantation. After Lucy, her son Robert, served as postmaster, making a total of 19 years the Howlett family officially handled the mail at Howlett Hall.

In September 1912 when William H. Taft was president, Walter Somers received appointment and moved the post office to the general merchandise store he had owned previously. The store sat near Green Point Wharf where steamers made port of call. According to "Buddy" Edwards in a 1983 interview, Curtis Chisley built the store. Somers, being an active businessman, also owned two schooners that hauled lumber, which was sawed by his mill, to Baltimore. The sawmill sat at the top of the hill, where in later years the Highway Department built Route 3 to accommodate Twigg Bridge. Quite an industrious fellow, Somers acquired a tomato-canning factory from Jim Tobin. It sat on the west side of the ferry dock. He brought immigrants, who were Bohemians, but acted like gypsies, from Baltimore to assist in the operation of the sawmill and the canning factory. Somers built a camp in the woods west of the sawmill where these workers lived during the season of their employment. He paid the immigrants with due bills, redeemable only at the general store. Their wages paid for groceries and other purchases. Any amount that they didn't use was carried over until the next week. They never saw cash since Somers deposited their wages at the store.

Somers sold his store to John Andrew Twigg from Baltimore in 1908 according to his grandson, Wallace B. Twigg. In 1911, Twigg started a ferry service from Green Point to Lundeen's Farm in Middlesex County. That first ferry was only a row skiff that Twigg probably built himself. In short time, a lighter, a small gasoline engine boat attached to a barge-like boat by pivot point, made the crossing. The ferry tender was summoned from the opposite shore by either blowing a loud horn or hoisting a flag up a pole by day. A lantern told him to come for a passenger at night. An adjustable ramp would be lowered at each shore for boarding and departing. Later Twigg built a new wharf for the ferry to land, placing it a distance from the steamer wharf. Huge oil tanks still stand in the space between the two wharfs. Floyd and W. R. Thompson had a franchise with the BP Oil Company, who installed the tanks.

When Twigg died in 1930, the family sold the ferry service to Curtis and Willis Chisley and William Lundeen, according to what Curtis Fitchett told a *Gloucester-Mathews Gazette-Journal* reporter in 1983. Fitchett had piloted the ferry for 27 years. Foster Oliver purchased the service from the three owners, operating it until the state took over the operation in 1939. It is uncertain what year, the ferry with the inboard engine came into use, but that is what I traveled on in past years. One needed to know the schedule to arrive in time for the ferry that had a regular run. What a disappointment to arrive at the dock, seeing the ferry pulling out. It was an hour's wait. "Oh No!" would be the exclamation of everyone in the car.

When the state built the John Andrew Twigg Bridge in 1953, the ferry service ended. There was a grand celebration with marching bands and speeches, honoring Twigg the day of the ribbon cutting. In later years, residents realized the convenient bridge brought about the death of

Dixie as a place to gather mail and shop while visiting neighbors.

The estate house, where the post office sat in those early years, carried the original name of "Providence" under the ownership of Mr. and Mrs. McComb. But they sold it more than thirty years later to Mr. And Mrs. Hope Norton, who called the estate "Hopemont." After Norton died, she found it necessary to sell the property and to this day, it is again known by its original name "Providence."

Dixie Post Office, which served the area that had originally made up Providence Plantation, moved from the store to its own building when they built Route 3 for Twiggs Bridge. The small post office sat to one side of Route 3, now Twiggs Ferry Road, adjoining the Sadler property. Rebecca V. Edwards, known as Virginia, retired with Dixie Post Office closing December 31, 1968. Mail went to Cobbs Creek. While I operated "The Craftsman Shop," the business that my husband and I had established in 1952, I had several Middlesex County clients, who interestingly used Cobbs Creek Post Office as their mailing address. It had been convenient at Dixie—just a drive over the river. But they continued the trip to Mathews for mail. (Much of the information from the *Gloucester-Mathews Gazette-Journal* April 4,1983.)

Actions not only speak louder than words—they often obviate the need of words." (The Richardson Review, April 1927)

Dixie Post Office 1983

Picture courtesy the Mathews-Gloucester Gazette-Journal

Cardinal Post Office Established

"Love in a letter endures forever in our memories.
Emily Post

In 1895, the community south of Foster Post Office and north of Bohannon on East River Road felt need of their own post office with the increased population. Time involved in the walk, or even to hitch the horse to a wagon and make the trip, to either of the other post offices seemed unnecessary. After all, a general merchandise store sat on the corner of East River Road and what is now Cardinal Road. So Robert B. Gayle applied to the Post Office Department for such an office. No one really knows who thought of the name, but since the woodland in the community to this day is filled with cardinals, the residents feel the birds initiated it. In November of that year, Gayle received appointment for a post office to be located in the store.

Whether Gayle owned the store, no one is certain. However, 83-year-old Nellie Mae Anderton remembers John Vernon Hearn, known as Vernon, owning the store in her childhood days when he served as postmaster. He had been appointed in October 1914. Hearn grew up on "Oakland Farm" on North River Road near the intersection of Cardinal Road. When I talked with Anderton, she said Vernon's family lived above the store. Hearn served as postmaster thirty-two years, retiring the end of March 1946.

I found little information in print about Cardinal Post Office. The one thing I did find was from the *Mathews Journal,* March 3, 1910, tells that Cardinal neighbors had erected a building for a library building. "A building 24 by 30 feet, nearly every family in the radius of three or four miles has contributed to its building and furnishing. It is an old-fashioned log cabin in the woods with a broad hospitable fireplace and comfortable chairs. Now we have the building built and paid for, we want some books to fill it."

Anderton remembers a garage near the store on East River Road before 1930 until the latter part of the twentieth century. Whether there had been a wheelwright and blacksmithing business earlier is probable but uncertain.

Richard Edgar Paul, known as Edgar, operated the store and became postmaster upon Hearn's retirement. In the 1960s, the store closed and the post office moved to its own small building, closer to North River Road. It closed temporarily in 2004 due to unsafe conditions. If a suitable location isn't found in proper time, the closure will become permanent. Mail has gone to North, Foster and Bohannon Post Offices, according to where the patrons live.

"While traveling by train, one rider found himself sitting by a millionaire. When the passenger inquired how being a

millionaire felt, his seatmate replied: "I have no comprehension of just what a million means... My experience, however, has taught me that the joy and sunshine of life are the results of my mental attitude towards things of which I am conscious and can see." The Richardson Review, April 1927

Soles the Northernmost Post Office in the County

Package of Old Letters

In a little rosewood casket that is resting on the stand is a package of old letters written in a faded hand.

1930s Scrapbook Clipping

Residents began to build more houses in the community known as Morgan's Branch, located near the intersection of Route 3, Windsor Road, and Route 198, the northernmost end of Buckley Hall Road. Morgan's Branch obtained its name, being the end of "a stream in the south west of the community's crossroads and flows into 'Wading Creek,' which empties into the Piankitank River." (*Gloucester-Mathews Gazette-Journal* August 16, 1984)

In 1897 Charles C. Soles built his general merchandise store in front of his home, "Racefield," a distance from the intersection. Once he became established, he applied for a post office since it was a three mile walk or wagon ride to Cobbs Creek Post Office, where he and his customers fetched their mail. Soles was appointed postmaster on November 2, 1897.

In the Mathews County Historical Society's archives with the *Gloucester-Mathews Gazette-Journal's* clippings, I found quotes by Soles' daughter, the late Mrs. Charles Edwards. She said that local storekeepers were akin to reporters back in the days before modern conveyances. Soles became the center of communications for the neighborhood.

Only two newspapers came to the post office since no house-to-house delivery existed in those days. The *Baltimore American* had a whole page of funnies each week. With no school nearby, many residents never learned to read. Soles had been fortunate enough to receive his education at Cobbs Creek School and felt sorry for the illiterate. To give them a laugh, he let a woman known as Aunt Flossie read the funnies aloud on Saturday nights. A crowd gathered for her readings, bending double with laughter as Aunt Flossie mimicked each character presented effectively.

Although many couldn't read more than their names, they knew simple figures. A merchant never gave one of the illiterate the wrong change, or they'd catch the cheat. Parents managed to pass figures and denominations of money from generation to generation. Each knew how many eggs it took to purchase a pound of sugar, etc.

Mrs. Edwards told about the time her father went to Baltimore to buy for the store, coming back with a pair shoes for her. He had paid $3 for them, causing the entire neighborhood to declare him crazy with extravagance.

At a later date, Soles moved the store up the road to the corner. He sold it to William J. Grimstead in 1905. However, Soles still worked in the store for several years until Grimstead added the living quarters to the back of the store. In time, Grimstead rented the building to Nelson and Emory Haynes, who operated their own general merchandise store for a time.

Bailey Adams married Grimstead's daughter and purchased the store from his father-in-law in the early 1930s when Herbert Hoover was president. They rented the upstairs rooms to traveling "drummers," who spent the night before resuming their sales pitches to more merchants in Mathews and Gloucester Counties.

Meanwhile, the post office had remained in the store until April 1918, but was discontinued at that time. It was reinstated in another building on Windsor Road in May 1922 with Clyde Kemp as postmaster. When he retired in June 1940, it closed and mail went to Dutton Post Office in Gloucester. Mail still goes to Mathews' residents at Dutton with Highway Carrier delivery to their homes.

Picture Courtesy of the *Gloucester-Mathews Gazette-Journal*

Soles Post Office, after porch had been enclosed, stood on the corner of Routes 3 and 198.

Warehouse Post Office

"I count only the sunny hours." Sundial Motto

Minor B. Matthews built his empire at the end of Route 631, Chapel Lane, on the Piankitank. He had built a house, where Matthews, his wife and daughter Mary lived, with a store and warehouse attached. Near the close of 1897, he felt need of a post office in his general merchandise store. The Baltimore Steamer already stopped at the wharf twice a week, bringing supplies and mail. The Post Office Department approved his application and appointed Matthews as postmaster at Warehouse Post Office in January 1898.

J. T. Christian also had an oyster warehouse at Warehouse Wharf. The sign over the door read: "Planter & Shipper of Fine Salt Water Oysters--Warehouse Wharf."

According to the National Archives, Matthews served as postmaster from the date that the post office was established until his last days. He died November 11, 1930, but the family managed the post office until January 1931 when it closed. Mail went to Blakes.

In an interview with Kathryn Haynes, who has lived in the area for years, I learned that the Matthews' family continued to occupy the house. Their only child, Mary, married Rev. Bland Taylor and they had a daughter, Helen. When Mary and Taylor had divorced, she married a Mr. De Simone. Though it wasn't occupied continually, the family still owned the building through the years. In the 1960s, Helen, by then a Clark, taught at Mathews High School and lived at the home place. She befriended her neighbors, the senior Carmeans. Kathryn often saw her at their home, where Helen related much about the earlier days at Warehouse Wharf. When Helen came home from school to find the tide had risen due to northeast winds, she couldn't always cross an area between the cove and the river, where it cut the house off. "And neither Grandpa or Papa were there to fix it." So Helen spent the night with neighbors. When she left the county that time, she moved to a northwestern state.

Though there were other owners before them, today Dr. and Mrs. Leigh Budwell have a beautiful home in the restored building. I visited the Budwells on a blustery Saturday afternoon. The entrance to the house, that section having been totally rebuilt, faces the Piankitank River, where the wind blew my hair straight back as I walked into the breeze. In 1898, the shoreline would have been much farther from the house since every storm has taken a bit of the land before the Budwells built the bulkhead and installed rip raft.

Though the living quarters of the building is new, the original store and warehouse stand, beautifully restored. The original ceiling and sidewalls of the store took my eye with its herringbone construction. The shelving remains on the long back wall, filled from ceiling to floor with Indian artifacts, items from the river such as small and large shark's teeth, conch shells and remains of other sea life. There are also antique dental tools the retired dentist enjoys and collectibles from the states and China. Black iron pots and kettles adorn the top shelf. It would take hours to detail the whole display. They removed the shelves from the opposite wall to install windows for view of the River. A door in the center of the shelves takes you down one step into the original warehouse, where Dr. Budwell has a workshop, creating sculptures among other things.

A steep stairway leads to the original balcony, which displays larger antiques. The original spokes on the railing reveal more of the Victorian period. The Budwells filled the steps with copper kettles and other appropriate memorabilia, making sure no one falls climbing the steep steps. Thieves made way with the thick black walnut counter while Dr. and Mrs. Budwell were still living in Richmond and coming to the house whenever possible to inspect or do restoration.

From the Budwell's yard, I could see Iron Point to the east and Roane's Point to the west, and he pointed to the Chesapeake Bay far out beyond the Piankitank River. Water from the river wraps the original entrance to the store, forming a large cove in the back of the house and southeastward. The area is known as "Warehouse Cove" today.

"When we limit our thinking, we limit our expression."
The Richardson Review July-August 1927

Warehouse Post Office, the porch has been replaced with an open deck. However the shelves remain on one wall stocked with antiques and collectibles. The walls and floor are original with the herringbone design standing out where it has been used.

Susan Post Office Established

"Just a Word"

"T'was easy to say that I would write,
But 'tis hard to find the time;
And I know you're waiting to hear from me,
So I'll simply send this rhyme."
Post Card 1911

Records show the county divided into Townships in the nineteenth century. Below Mathews Court House was known as Chesapeake Township, according to census records. William Larkin Williams, descendent of Samuel Williams, at Williams Wharf, lived south of Port Haywood Post Office. Known as Larkin Williams, the lame merchant married a Miss Ransone. Larkin and his family operated a store that was attached to their two-story house in the 1890s.

In December 1897, Larkin Williams wrote a letter to the Assistant Postmaster General in Washington D.C. He requested a post office be established between Port Haywood and New Point. The reply informed him to select a short name for the proposed office which, when written, would not resemble the name of any other post office in the state.

Williams received his appointment dated February 15, 1898 as postmaster of Susan Post Office. Some say he named the office for his sister, Susan Mildred Williams. However, most I interviewed believe it was named for his daughter, Susan Williams, who married an Odell. The office sat in the corner of Williams General Merchandise Store. It remained in that building, with three of his daughters, Susan, Ellen, and Lucy, each serving as postmasters after his itinerary of over 25 years. Lucy Williams Hudgins retired in March 1955.

The store had been closed so the post office moved to Cecil F. Smith General Store, occupying a small cubicle in the front corner. William C. Pugh served as acting postmaster until September 1956. It was retired for three months and mail went to Port Haywood. When it was reinstated in December of the same year, Jane G. Brooks served as postmaster. Other postmasters served until Smith's store burnt in 1968. "The office temporarily moved to Port Haywood where the postmaster shared a small area in that office until the present building was built." (Most information taken from a flyer by the Annie Laura Goin, Postmaster October 1972 until 2000.)

The new building sat on the opposite side of the highway from Smith's store. In February 1998, Goin hosted the Century celebration of Susan Post Office. She wrote on the handout sheets, "I'm very proud to be a part of our great postal service and to be of service to the community where I was born. I look forward to meeting my customers each day as each has become very special to me during my twenty-five years of service. I feel that we are one big family."

In 2004, Helen Hurst, another lifetime resident, serves as postmaster. I also interviewed Dianne G. Hudgins, Assistant Postmaster, after my conversation with Hurst. I learned that in 2004, the post office has 95 post office boxes, 71 of which are rented, 36 families receive their mail by highway carrier on the Star Route and 13 receive general delivery like in the old days.

The original building where Susan Post Office first sat still stands with the warehouse on the side. I could see that shelves still remained on the sidewalls from the road. Carole Thomason owns the home and store today, operating a small bed and breakfast. She plans to make a sitting room of the store building in the future. The Williams family would be proud to see their home place operating still as a business.

Penny Post Office on Bethel Beach Road

"One of the large speed vans of our National Transfer Company will take the furnishings from a six room home at one load and take it any distance for 80c. a mile."
The Richardson Review July-August 1927, referring to my Great-Uncle Fred Richardson's company.

"Robert Brownley, age 19, and his cousin, Grayson Armistead, age 21, decided to try their luck with general merchandise business." (The *Gloucester-Mathews Gazette-Journal* February 20, 1986) They had their store building on the corner of Routes 609, Bethel Beach Road, and 608, Potato Neck Road. Since the nearest post office was a good distance from the location, the 200 residents needed a post office closer home. Armistead had just had his 21st birthday (the legal age for a postmaster), but they applied in his father's name, Augustus L. Armistead, known as "Buck." He received official appointment on February 27, 1899 with Penny Post Office as the name.

The younger men served in the store and post office, taking turns. The *Gloucester-Mathews Gazette-Journal* reported outside of the store a large sign stood. It was a colored woman with a handkerchief around her head, reading: "MAXWELL HOUSE COFFEE—GOOD TO THE LAST DROP." ("Colored" was the appropriate term in that day.)

Merchandise for the store had to picked up from Diggs Wharf where Captain Coffee delivered on the Norfolk Steamer. In1903 Grayson A. Armistead applied for the post office in his name and became the official postmaster.

Seven years later, Robert Brownley drowned, dissolving the partnership. Circumstances didn't allow Armistead to continue with the enterprise so the store and post office closed. When I interviewed Margaret Armistead, I learned that her father, Jessie Hutson, purchased the store building, moving it to his property farther down Potato Neck. Armistead and Hutson ran the business. Hutson's daughter, Margaret, and Armistead's son, William, married some years later.

Those folk had to travel back to Laban to fetch their mail for three months before Peary Post Office was established.

"In 1831 the Postmaster at Hammondsville, Ohio, reported: 'On a letter one hundred miles and over, five dozen eggs, or five pounds butter, or two bushels of oats, or two bushels of potatoes, or two-thirds of a bushel of wheat; and thirty-two such letters a good milch cow.'" The Richardson Review July-August 1927

Shell Post Office

> *"My Volumes of Good Wishes,*
> *For thee, dare I unfold them,*
> *Would cover such a space me thinks,*
> *No Library would hold them."*
> Post Card 1916

Little can be found about the post office to which Raymond J. Mattox was appointed postmaster on March 4, 1899. The location, described as three miles south of North Post Office on his application, definitely had a warehouse at or near Auburn Wharf according to all the older residents that I contacted. We do not know if the post office sat in the corner of the warehouse, or was it in a separate small building. No one remembers hearing of a general merchandise store at the location. According to the National Archives, Mattox requested "Auburn" as the name for his office, but the department denied his request. Why they named it "Shell" is your guess. Oyster shells reinforced most of the shorelines near the wharfs so my guess: "Shell" could refer to the shell road leading to the office.

Charles Heath received his appointment in May 1903, serving until January 1912 when the post office closed.

Robert Hicks, now in his eighties, having spent his lifetime near Auburn, said that he had heard his father and grandfather speak of Shell Post Office and meeting the steamer at the warehouse. Sallie Anne, his wife, moved from a Pennsylvania city to the Hicks' property when they married in the 1950s. So she said that she had to learn a whole new way of life.

The young Mrs. Hicks learned to put an eight-quart-covered container of milk in the refrigerator after straining it mornings. When she removed the container, she skimmed the thick cream off the top, saving it for butter. Once in awhile a bit of the cream was taken out and put aside when a dessert needed whipped cream. It must be enough to make the tasty dish—but not to be whipped too long or it would become butter, according to Mrs. Hicks. Then she poured the milk into bowls to clabber. Once when the milk wouldn't clabber after the cow came fresh (had a new calf), Sallie Anne contacted the county agent to learn that feed with preservatives, like pasteurized milk, prevented clabbering. The senior Mrs. Hicks had also taught her how to make cottage cheese among other things. One didn't need to waste any part of the milk.

The evening milk was strained and put into bottles for drinking or other table use, including cooking. She ordered caps to put on the milk bottles from Sears, Roebuck and Company's catalogue. One needed to shake the bottle before removing the cap to mix the milk and cream evenly. Sometimes the Hicks couple reached into the full bottle with a spoon to have just cream in their coffee.

Sallie Anne learned to use eggs for the groceries that they didn't have on the farm. She became intrigued with the credit and debit columns in the grocer's account book. He mailed the hand-copied record to the family once a month until she told him that it wasn't necessary.

Mrs. Hicks expressed admiration for the African-American, whom she knew as Capt. John Billups. He left his car at the Hicks' place when he went out in his boat to tong oysters. When Mrs. Hicks left him a note on his car seat, concerning something that she had for him to take home for the evening meal, she was surprised that Capt. John left without it. Later, she learned that he had to take the note home to have his wife read it to him.

An interesting story that Sallie Anne Hicks related concerned her subscription to the *Reader's Digest.* Before she married, she had taken a lifetime membership to the magazine for $25—a fair sum in that day. A short time before the wedding, she notified them of what her new name and address would be. Actually, a copy of the magazine arrived at North Post Office before the ceremony and her move. She continues to receive Reader's Digest as per the agreement. What a bargain!

"I wish to complain," said the bride haughtily, "about the flour you sold me. It was tough." "Tough, Ma'am?" asked the grocer. "Yes, tough, I made a pie with it, and my husband could hardly cut it." The Richardson Record July-August 1927 quoted as written from *Progressive Grocer*

Retz Post Office in the Glebe

Be Honest

*"If you cannot give your employer your best effort,
Make room for someone who will."*
Post Card 1916

The area southwest of Mathews Court House became known as the "Glebe" in the early days of the county's history. Justus F. Retz, a German immigrant and shoemaker, purchased property for his home from George Greene in the western side of this short but wide neck in November 1878. Retz had married Alice Jarvis from Cow Neck on the western side of the county so looked for land to build a home in the county prior to the wedding.

James Polke Blake operated his general merchandise store in the Glebe and realized they needed a post office. He applied early in 1899, receiving his appointment on April 7th of that year. No one knows why he asked for the name "Retz," but being different and short, the officials accepted it. Some descendents of residents interviewed in January 1983 by a *Gloucester-Mathews Gazette-Journal* reporter believe mail had been delivered in the area before this date although the National Archives Registry shows no record of it. Did Retz pick up bundles for residents near him with his own mail and hand it out from his cobblers shop? If so, the name seems appropriate.

Retz Post Office served a diversity of citizens: Farmers, seagoing men, doctors, carpenters, businessmen, lawyers and wheelwrights through the years. In 1983, Duffy Marchant told a *Gazette-Journal* reporter that his father was an agent for Hoskins Lumber Company of Baltimore earlier in the century. The senior Mr. Marchant had to scout out good timberland, buying it for the company. He was responsible to see that the trees were cut and delivered to Baltimore, after having made the purchase. After the men felled the trees, they were hauled to the nearest river and loaded on rafts. Depending on their size, 900 to 2,000 logs made up a raft, and a tugboat pulled as many as three rafts. They traveled up the Chesapeake Bay to Baltimore. His biggest difficulty was getting the rafts from the shallow rivers to the tugboat. It took a bit of careful planning.

Small boats took bushels of oysters, barrels or crates of beans, peas and potatoes for sale in Baltimore or Norfolk to meet the steamboats when they arrived in the deeper rivers or small bays. Only a few traveled on the winding-bumpy roads through woodlands to the steamboat's wharf.

Frederick Richardson, who was my great grandfather, had a home in the Glebe, as did his ancestors from the eighteenth century. His place sat on a cove off East River. He and his wife, Elizabeth Susan White Richardson, had seven children—six boys and one girl. Mary Josephine (Molly) remained in the county while the sons moved to Richmond and Norfolk. Most owned their own businesses, and the others did well in their choice of employment. My granddaddy, Melvin, was the youngest and became a toolmaker. He made intricate small tools and parts by hand—a very tedious work. He found demand for his work in shipyards, railroad yards, and Langley Air Force Base hired him after he retired from the Newport News Shipyard. Although he apprenticed in Norfolk, he lived in the county for some years, commuting home on weekends. Later he rented homes in Hampton, living in a new house on Cherokee Road the longest. After Granny died, he moved to my aunt's home on Fitchetts Wharf Road where he spent his last days.

Besides the Richardson family, there were Thurstons, Miles, Marchants, Greenes, Gayles, Treakles, among names of prominent residents, living in the Glebe in the nineteenth century.

The children studied in private schools before buses took them to Lee Jackson School in Mathews. Duffy Marchant had gone to the second private school that existed in his neighborhood near the post office.

The post office remained in Blake's store with Blake serving as postmaster three different times. After his first two years, Blake operated the office in between Callis and Miles, serving for 12 years. Then he was reinstated in between Greene and Baker for seven years. Politics seemed to have brought the changes. In 1926, Mrs. Bessie Maude Hurst became postmaster and moved the office to its own small building on the corner of Routes 622, Long Road, and 623, Greene Road. In 1930, Melvin Thurston, having become postmaster moved it a short distance again. He retired in 1945, but Mabel Hall served from the same site until it closed in November 1953. Mail went to Mathews Post Office.

"Postal rates on letters to a bank in 1831: On a single letter for a distance of thirty miles 6½c, five times that distance if the letter weighed over one ounce and contained more than

one closure, $1.00. The Richardson Review July-August
1927

Picture courtesy Mary Cannon Godsey, who now lives in North Carolina.
Someone in South Carolina furnished her with the picture.

Retz Post Office in the Glebe

Chapter Seven

"To My Friend"
"When the candle casts its shadows around your downy bed,
And you're feeling Oh, so browsy,
And evening prayers are said,
Think once, think twice—Think oftener if you will
Of one who ne'er forgets you, a friend who loves you still."
Post card 1915

Hallieford Post Office in Cow Creek

According to the older residents, Cow Neck folk gave the cattle credit for shaping the winding road from Blakes to the water in the 1800s and before. The crooked and rugged path through woodlands caused one woman's horse to break its leg when stepping in a hole. Someone came and shot the horse where it fell. Water bordered Cow Neck on three sides. So in time of drought, the cattle that ran on the commons with bells around their necks traveled towards the water where the grass grew greener. Those residents told that the cows traveled in herds, being noisy with every bell ringing. However thirst dominated. And the salty creeks and rivers weren't fit for man or beast to drink. So after rains, all the cows headed for the bottomless pond off Route 626, Hallieford Road, first. The cows would congregate around the edge of the pond, drinking as if it meant life or death. Speaking of the neck to a *Gloucester-Mathews Gazette-Journal* reporter in 1982, 70-year-old Tinsley Morse said, "Solid full of people when I came along." When I visited and interviewed Dorothy White, she spoke about the cows and their bells in Cow Neck. I feel she spoke of conversations with older folk in the neighborhood in her younger years. (On recent larger county maps, the Pond is shown before the turn into Skipjack Lane.)

Robert H. Matthews had built his large house by 1900. It sat on the corner of Route 626, Hallieford Road, and Route 681, Burton Point Road. But the populace lived on down the roads near the water on the three sides of Cow Neck, making the trek to Blakes to retrieve their mail a bit long. Why couldn't they have a post office? Early in the twentieth century, Matthews sent his application to the Assistant Post Office General. Meanwhile, he built a shed from which Hallie Matthews would operate his office. He took her name, adding "ford," for the name of the office— thus "Hallieford."

General merchandise stores were scattered about Cow Neck on convenient corners. Around 1930 there were five such stores in operation, allowing residents easy access to trade for items they couldn't produce themselves. Most walked through the rugged cow and wagon paths that the few trucks and cars had found rather hazardous. The residents worked in the water while others went to sea. Morse knew that "more steamboat captains came out of Hallieford than any other place in the U. S. for its size." Another elderly resident in 1982, Benita Morris, said her husband, the late Thomas J. Morris, was a tugboat captain, working one week and off one week. His father, the late James Morse, was cook on the same shift on a tugboat.

Means of livelihoods for the residents included one mail carrier, who traveled in his buggy. Hallie Matthews also operated an oyster house; a marine railway kept the workboats operating in good order; two blacksmith shops stayed busy shoeing horses and mending broken wagons and buggies; a cobbler's shop that sat on the far side of Broaddus store kept soles on shoes; and the Morris family raised and sold jonquils. With each family raising their own gardens, chickens and usually one or more pigs for fall slaughter, they kept busy.

Ronnie Broaddus, postmaster until December 2003, represented the friendliness of the community when he greeted a neighbor, old or new, in the store or post office. Like the music he played in church on Sunday, he soothed and encouraged in his own mild manner, making one feel welcome. Unless someone needed help with their mail, he had time to tell me about the community that he'd known since birth on my several visits to the office. Never a negative word.

Hallieford residents saw that their children received an education when they built a private school across from the location of Broaddus Store. The community built the school and hired Annie Ashburn as teacher. Sitting under a grove of trees, the school also served as a community hall for public events like church socials. Any denomination could use the building. The colored children attended New Hope School in Blakes in those days. Later children went to public schools in the county on school buses. (The Afro-American children preferred to be called "colored" in that day.)

In the mid 1970s, Hallieford's population grew when an enterpriser developed the subdivision, known as Sail Cove. It brought many new families from as far away as New York, Boston and retired military service personnel from several parts of the United States. Many of the lots bordered the edge of Queen's Creek, and the folks in the early part of the century would have spoken of the houses as "fine." Ronnie Broaddus said, "How they found out about Hallieford, I don't know." While 90-year-old Bessie Morse stated, "almost new community. Don't know hardly anybody."

Yet, the newcomers were welcomed. Some stated, "We never felt not wanted". Virginia Greene, from near Mathews Court House, married in the 1940s, moving to Hallieford, near her husband's family. She spoke of life in the community in 1982, saying she had spent "34 glorious years at Hallieford". She continued, "The more neighbors that come, the better they get."

Postmasters changed over the years. Records tell us that the post office moved a few times before it found its final home place in Elmo Broaddus' store. Broaddus' wife, Marie served as postmaster from April 1938 until May 1976. Her son Ronald, known as "Ronnie," assisted her in the later years. Ronald E. Broaddus became full time postmaster when his mother retired and worked in that capacity until his unexpected death in December 2003. Virginia Owens, his assistant, served in the post office for a time, but Kathy Sadler is postmaster today. In 1938 the post office served 75 families, and by 1982 Broaddus served 90 families. Today, many receive their mail in boxes in front of their homes by highway carrier on Cobbs Creek's Star Route. But an interview with Virginia Owens revealed that Hallieford Post Office has 96 boxes and 64 families, receiving general delivery in the old fashioned manner until the post office can obtain more boxes. The figures show rapid growth where cows once roamed among few residents.

On February 16, 2001, Ronnie Broaddus, postmaster, and Virginia Owens, assistant postmaster, hosted a hundredth birthday party for Hallieford Post Office. They gave souvenirs and served tasty home baked treats to all, who gathered for the observance. Ronnie enjoyed people and making them feel welcome.

It's the welcome that folks find, which makes Cow Neck such a friendly place during retirement or to live a lifetime. Folks from urban locations learn to live life at a slower pace with time to chat at the post office or to run next door.

(Information gleaned from several interviews and September 23, 1982 in the *Gloucester-Mathews Gazette-Journal* article.)

Hallieford Post Office in the 1980s when the store with the post office in the right front corner flourished. The office now sits on the right facing the building

Redart Post Office in Crab Neck

"They that can give up essential liberty to obtain a little temporary safety deserve neither liberty nor safety."
Benjamin Franklin

William N. Trader, who had applied for two post offices previously, saw need for one near his home, "Point Breeze," on Milford Haven by 1901. At that time the community spoke of him as Captain Trader. Since the second post office, he had applied for was "Trader," he reversed the name, applying for "Redart."

The land located between Stutts Creek and Milford Haven had been known as Crab Neck as far back as anyone recalls. In a 1990 interview with a *Gloucester-Mathews Gazette-Journal* reporter, Rachel Hunley Nabor said, "My grandfather told me at one time only Lillys, Callises and Hunleys lived in Crab Neck. The Traders were 'squatters.' They squatted on Callis land."

"The Hunleys owned so much land on Stutts Creek," Lillie Godsey said to the reporter, "that the area was known as 'Hunleytown.'" Godsey said that the residents made a living by harvesting the Bay from sunrise to sunset, usually netting $1 a day. Most had small farms, from which they provided for their families. Captain L.M. Travis owned "Goshen" the largest and most profitable farm in the neck.

Nearly all of the residents received their mail at Cricket Hill, but those to the south of the neck found Hudgins nearer. In 1959, Josephine Carney Callis, who would soon have her 90th birthday, told Dorothy D. Foster that her family found traveling by boat to Fitchetts Post Office the most convenient for the mail before Redart Post Office was established. But when Stutts Creek froze solid for some weeks in winter months, she hitched the horse and buggy and drove across the creek to fetch the mail. Wonder how many more found the creek more desirable than the dusty or muddy roads?

The children in the area attended Cattail Branch School, a private school, which was in walking distance. It sat on a piece of land on Route 223, Cricket Hill Road, between Redart and Hudgins. Parents paid $1.00 per month for a student to attend the two-room schoolhouse, with a sliding door separating the rooms, which Miss Florie Callis operated. The first student, who arrived at the school in the morning, started the fire. The school closed when buses became available for transporting the students to larger schools. The building is gone, but Florie Callis' niece has built a home on the site. (Mildred Callis Tucker assisted me with this information.)

Crab Neck boasted a boatyard on Callis Creek, where Noah Foster built schooners in the 1800s. The inhabitants went in their boats to Hole-In-The-Wall for weenie roasts and picnics. Residents from both shores enjoyed the small island. In 1947, my parents, Maywood and Grace Callis, took my sister, my husband, Kirby, and me to the same site after we fished for a time in Daddy's workboat. Leaving Stutts Creek, we circled around Crab Neck toward Gwynns Island on Milford Haven. Then we went ashore at Hole-In-The Wall, where we roasted weenies and picnicked, sitting on a blanket and eating from the tablecloth and basket that Momma had packed for the occasion. I discovered that Daddy had wanted Kirby to know where his oyster shore beds lay when he asked us to plan the outing. Yet none of us enjoyed a day of fun more than Daddy.

A small Evangelical Friends Church held services for some years in Crab Neck. However in 1919, the building sat idle. Wilbur C. Diggs of Laban Post Office and several other residents, including Robert Hunley, who lived towards Mathews Court House on Pine Hall Road and had been a member of the church in Crab Neck, purchased the building for $20. They removed it piece-by-piece and built Peniel Evangelical Friends Church at Laban. The members donated the benches with the sale. (Information from files by Wilbur C. Diggs, founder and pastor of Peniel for 39 years.)

Captain Trader owned the store where Redart Post Office first sat with James W. Hudgins as postmaster as of November 1901. There were other postmasters after Hudgins served his 10 years, but the post office discontinued from mid-April until near the end of December in 1916. Mail went to Hudgins those months. William N. Trader had died at age 70 in April 1914 so his store either had sold or was for sale. When the post office reopened, Edgar A. Foster served as postmaster for the next six years. It was two years after he left the post office that he joined in partnership with his brother, Wilbur, in the establishment of the only department store Mathews ever had, Foster's, Inc. in Mathews Court House.

In May 1926, after Charles Harris Williams term of almost four years, the post office closed and mail went to Cricket Hill Post Office. But John R. "Romie" Tabor purchased and operated Trader's store, becoming postmaster in August 1931. Eight years later, Vaden Wise purchased the store and served as postmaster until he retired in 1961. Mary Callie Callis assisted him. After his retirement, Nellie Mae Owens was acting postmaster until her husband, James Langley Owens, known as "Bud," became postmaster. Owens built a new store and post office in 1963 where the post office remained until it closed in January 1993 with only 75 customers remaining. (Bud Owens assisted me with missing information.)

Redart Post Office last sat in the store that "Bud" Owens built.

Wonder what Trader would have thought or said if he had received the bundle of labels Bud Owens opened in 1990? They read "Redheart," Virginia.

William: "Are you sure your wife knows I'm going home to dinner with you?" Johnson: "Knows! I should say so! Why, dear man, I argued with her about it this morning for half an hour!" The Richardson Record June 1927

Tabernacle Post Office

"A Suggestion
Let me tell you in two minutes
You could pencil just a line
Here I send you an example
In these hurried words of mine."
Post card 1917

The Methodist Episcopal Churches on the Mathews Charge, which included Central, Salem, Bethel and St. Matthews churches, built a bush-arbor tabernacle by the summer of 1882. It sat on the side of Route 611, Tabernacle Road, across from the intersection of, Salem Church Road. In July, open-air meetings were more comfortable for evangelistic services than stuffy churches. Meetings lasted two weeks with a visiting evangelist and song leader— evening services, all day service on Sundays and some weekdays. When the services lasted all day, the members packed picnic baskets. In time the first tabernacle burnt, and they built an open-sturdy-framed tabernacle. Today, owned by Mr. And Mrs. Robert C. Hutson, it stands as a historical landmark.

A community, called "The Ridge," had already existed in the area, two miles south of Mathews Court House. John M. Forrest, known as "Jack" Forrest, operated a store, facing Salem Church Road, on the corner across from the tabernacle. His two-story home sat in the large yard just past the store. Since customers lived in the nearby community and another mile southeast of the tabernacle without easy access to a post office, Forrest applied, requesting "Ridge" for his office. The Post Office Department denied him the name, but approved a second request for Tabernacle Post Office. His post office officially opened in March 1902. John's son Freddie W. Forrest became postmaster in March 1914.

From the 1920s, Freddie operated a wholesale candy business from the back of the store. The younger Forrest became a "drummer" to Mathews County's and surrounding counties' general merchandise stores, delivering the goods, for which, he had taken orders. It was November 1920 when John Forrest, became postmaster for the second time. Freddie's wife, Elsie Banks Forrest, accepted the position of postmaster in April 1930, serving 14 years. Elsie had actually been assistant postmaster much of the time after she and Freddie married, doing the work while the men only signed the reports.

In 1944, Elsie Forrest felt need to leave her position and move to her parents' home to help care for them. So the post office moved to a small building on the corner where Route 611 makes a sharp turn to the right with Tabernacle Road ending, becoming Garden Creek Road and Knight Wood Road intersects to the left. Arthur C. Hudgins served as postmaster with his daughter, Lois, assisting him before Lois became the official postmaster in July. She served until July 1955, having to retire due to physical conditions. Tabernacle was discontinued July 6, 1955. Mail went to Mathews and Diggs Post Offices with most residents on the Diggs Star Route.

In an interview with Ernest Callis, Jr., known as "Junior," he confirmed my belief that all the boys, whom he grew up with, were gone. He told what fun the group had after they completed their chores when out of school. The bunch of six boys would walk the miles to Jack Dutton's store at the entrance to Fitchett's Wharf Road, buying BB-Bats, a taffy-like candy on a sucker stick, for a penny. "We didn't do anything bad," Junior said. "Just played around and had a good time as we walked." Another day, they'd walk in the opposite direction to Ed Sadler's store at Beaverlette and buy more BB-Bats. In those days, these children didn't need to go to a nature museum to see butterflies, bees, birds, frogs or many other species of wild life. They studied them while walking. I attended school with Junior and most of the other boys that he mentioned. Like me, they learned the birdcalls, watched for tadpoles to hatch into frogs, and learned the habits of rabbits and squirrels. They watched the changes of a caterpillar into a butterfly, which would lay more eggs to begin the process over, and it became one of the most fascinating studies. The boys didn't think of these things as learning, but just growing to be a man. We talk about them as "the good old days."

Callis assisted me with information about Tabernacle in the earlier days.

Tabernacle Post Office sits in a neighbor's yard with a shed attached today. Unlike the original, it's small.

Moon Post Office

"The near-sighted man and his wife were inspecting the latest art exhibit with critical care.' That's the ugliest portrait, I've ever seen,' he said angrily, striving vainly for a better view of the abomination. 'Come away, you fool!" replied his wife. "You are looking at yourself in a mirror.'"
The Richardson Review June 1927

William Jefferson Callis built his general merchandise store where Fitchetts Wharf Road intersected with Rt. 198, and it became Haven Beach Road. It sat on a lot next to his home but nearer the road. Callis had his store well stocked and operating when he applied for a post office. He requested "Jeff" as the name for his office, but the Post Office Department denied him the name. According to the records in the National Archives, Callis said the mail arrived about midday so he suggested the name "Noon" on his second request. However, his handwriting, not being too plain, a gentleman in the department read it as "Moon." And so Moon Post Office became official on December 8, 1902.

Sitting well over a mile to the east of Mathews Post Office, a mile north of Fitchetts Wharf and being two miles west of Diggs Post Office, Moon Post Office became popular to both the Afro-Americans and the white population in the tightly knit community. Callis served as postmaster until age 69--over 30 years.

Charles E. Dutton, known as "Jack" Dutton, had purchased the business when he became postmaster in April 1931. Dutton served until a sudden illness cost him his life at age 50 in July 1942. His wife, Julia, and daughter, Helen, had assisted him in the post office the 11 years that he had served. Helen, by then Mrs. Russel Sadler, served as acting postmaster about two months until Marguerite R. Sadler received her appointment in October 1942. After Dutton's unexpected death, Howard Sadler had purchased the store business from the Duttons. The husband and wife team in the store and post office made an ideal situation.

Marguerite R. Sadler, who was my mother's sister, served as postmaster during the days of World War II when many airmail letters left the office and others arrived to and from the men both stateside and overseas. I had a part in this volume. I wrote my fiancé, Kirby, daily, but only mailed the letters two or three times a week since an airmail stamp cost six cents instead of the three cents that we usually paid for stamps. And when I insisted his Christmas gift go airmail to the Pacific arena, I really had to argue. It cost a whole $1.58—a lot in that day. But the ones that went regular parcel post seldom arrived Kirby had written. In 1945, he asked I keep any Christmas gift until he arrived home, or even better, I buy an item for our future home with the money. I don't remember what I did so my guess it was something to save for our house when that time arrived.

Howard Sadler closed the store, and Marguerite retired from post office duties by late October 1966. It was during Marguerite's vacation time the summer of 1966 that she spent days in the National Archives, researching Mathews Post Offices. She principally wanted the information for the Mathews County Historical Society, which she had helped establish. Marguerite stayed with a friend, whom she met when the Richardson family lived in Washington D.C., during her teen years.

Shirley Snow began her service as postmaster at Moon Post Office on October 26 of 1966 when Lyndon B. Johnson was president. I interviewed her while she worked in the office August 2004.

Mrs. Snow's busiest day in the post office was July 20, 1969, after the first manned spacecraft landed on the moon. How people across the United States and overseas found the tiny fourth-class office is anyone's guess. However, the deluge of mail poured in addressed to "Postmaster." There were approximately 2,500 requests for postmarks, according to *History and Progress, Mathews County, Virginia, published* by MCHS with reprints from the *Special Edition of the Gloucester-Mathews Gazette-Journal in 1979.* Two thousand of the requests came from an advertising firm in Chicago. Mrs. Snow thought postmark collecting a rare thing when an occasional visitor asked for one until that Memorial Day. She stamped letters all day, but took in little revenue since most envelopes came stamped. A second landing in the fall of that year brought more requests according to her. Shirley Snow not only has a postmarked envelope dated July 20, 1969, but also she has "a pretty good-sized b ox" packed full of requests for the postmark.

Picture courtesy my sister, Barbara Callis Bartha and my daughter, Susan Brooks Adams

Moon Post Office in late 1940s after World War II. The dark gray stripes of paint were painted during or just after 1945. The signs were typical of advertising in the 1930s and 1940s. Howard A. Sadler managed the store and Marguerite R. Sadler served as postmaster.

Due to conditions beyond her control, in April 2000 Mrs. Snow moved Moon Post Office from Jeff Callis's store, now an empty building under new ownership, to its own trailer with 238 locked post office boxes installed, giving room for growth. In August 2004, she reports 89 boxes rented and 40 families, receiving mail by highway carrier on the Star Route.

In 2003, one of her clients, who moved to the county in recent years and does ghost writing, with a post office box said, "I don't want them to ever close Moon Post Office. I meet people from about my neighborhood there, and Shirley is great." The client continued, "She will be retiring before too long, and I'll miss her."

Motorun Post Office

"A pair of good ears will drain dry a hundred tongues."
Benjamin Franklin

In April 1910, when William H. Taft had become the new president, John T. Davis felt need for another post office on Circle Drive. New Point Post Office seemed a bit too far for the growing community residents to travel for mail when a general merchandise store furnished other needs. The store was the nearest one to New Point Light House that had land not only for the attendant's home, but a beach and at one time a hotel. The late Thomas Gayle always said the sand on that beach was clean without a shell on it.

Sally Bett Walker Lawson told a *Gazette Journal* reporter in 1982 that groups from Mobjack traveled by way of an oyster boat to New Point Light House Beach for picnics. "There was beautiful beach there then," she said "There were dressing rooms and tables on a pier. In the afternoon we'd go for a swim and then come home by moonlight."

When Davis sought a different name than any in the state for his office, he remembered the sounds that had awakened him on recent weekday mornings. The fisherman, going out in their motorboats made far more noise than the oars that they had used in previous years. They surely run faster—so why not "Motorun." The Post Office Department accepted the unusual name. So on April 26, 1910, Davis stood proudly behind his new post office cage to receive and hand out mail for his patrons.

Norman C. Burroughs had built a general merchandise store, facing Circle Drive on the corner where the name changes to Lighthouse Road, intersecting New Point Comfort Highway. Burroughs sought the post office in 1916, under the administration of Woodrow Wilson, and received appointment in October, moving it from Davis' business. Motorun Post Office remained at that corner until 1928 when Stillman Hudgins sought and obtained appointment as postmaster. He moved it northwest to the corner where Circle Drive makes an abrupt turn.

Hudgins only kept the postmaster's position two months, according to residents, who said he turned it over to his assistant, Sadie Maude Thomas. She received the appointment as postmaster almost a year later in September 1929. Miss Thomas served in his store until it burned. After that, she erected a small building in the corner of her sister's yard, serving until her retirement in 1966 at age 70. On December 30th the post office closed, and mail went to Shadow. (Information from archives of *Gloucester-Mathews Gazette-Journal*)

Peary Post Office in Potato Neck

"No matter how smart you are, better have a good friend to tell you how dumb you really appear at times." The Richardson Review June 1927

Penny Post Office closed the end of January 1910. Three months later Arthur C. Hudgins acquired a post office farther down the area known as "Potato Neck" than Penny, which had been at the entrance to the neck. Laban Post Office had been a far distance for these folk to walk or travel by a horse drawn conveyance during the cold weather so they welcomed the new postmaster. Remember, winters used to be colder than they are today with deep snows and drifts, creeks froze over for weeks and even the Bay froze. Hudgins named his office for Rear-Admiral Robert Edwin Peary, who had discovered the North Pole the previous year. It sat in the corner of Alfred Tatterson's store. Tatterson had moved to the county with others of the family from Great Bay, New York between 1875 and 1880 according to W. B. Tatterson, Jr. Alfred Tatterson was known as "Captain Al".

Later in 1910, Clifford G. Hudgins, known as "Cliff," became the official postmaster, serving eight years. During this time, Captain Al had sold the store to Clifford Hudgins and Grayson A. Armistead. It carried the name Hudgins & Armistead. The store sat on Potato Neck Road where Peary Road intersects it. This placed the store and post office in the center of the community, convenient to all who left or came to the neck.

When I interviewed Miriam Thomas Callis, she described the older building. On the front, the store had a porch with a center door, having a window on either side on the first floor and one window on the second level. After entering the door, one had to go through swinging doors, the young folk of the community called "cowboy doors," to enter the main room. Here the post office sat in the right corner with the shelves, filled with merchandise, lining the long walls. Like other community stores of the day, one could purchase everything from baking soda to nails. To reach the second floor, you had to go up three steps, step on the counter and go up four more steps. The second level had shelves with pots and pans, men's wear for working on the water and other necessary items of that day. It probably wouldn't meet today's safety standards. But what building did in that day?

Grayson Armistead applied for postmaster, and the appointment became official in May 1918. Armistead served until March 31, 1949 when his son, William, accepted the position. Potato Neck residents no longer had to walk the miles to Laban Post Office.

Small farms sat on each side of Peary Road, many being on Horn Harbor on the east or an inlet off the Harbor on the west. If a family didn't have a workboat or skiff in back of their house, they had one at a neighbors or a public landing. Armistead, Smith, Hudgins, Thomas, Owens, Pugh and Hall were among some of the prominent names. They like folk in earlier communities made their living harvesting seafood from the Harbors and Chesapeake Bay. But these residents raised enough food on their small farms to feed the families and traded eggs and chickens for staple groceries—sugar, spices, baking powder, salt and anything that didn't grow locally.

Potato Neck residents traveled to the area of Laban Post Office to attend Bethel Methodist Episcopal Church. However in winter, the roads were too icy, especially on Wednesday evenings. Other than the physical danger with only lanterns for light, it was hard on the horses' hooves. So Miriam Callis' grandmother, Polly Ownings (later spelt Owens), gave a piece of land to build a chapel. The building, known as "Potato Neck Chapel," came under the authority of the Methodist Conference of Virginia. They met regularly on Wednesday evenings, being in walking distance of the homes in their neck. The chapel was also used to house Holly Grove School—a one-room schoolhouse. When the county built Winter Harbor School in the 1920s, the original building was donated to a needy family for a home.

By 1910 the community had grown and felt need for a permanent church closer home than Bethel. Arthur C. Hudgins donated land for the building, according to Callis's records. After several meetings with the officials at Bethel Methodist Church, the group was permitted to remove their membership. They called the new church St. Matthews Methodist Episcopal Church. The churches shared the same pastor. In fact, in those earlier years, one pastor served Central, Salem, Bethel and St. Matthews Methodist Episcopal churches. In later years, the charge was divided with more pastors—one serves Bethel and St. Matthews today.

On Potato Neck Road, houses sat on either side of the road, some with long lanes, carrying one through the woodland to the Harbor. Here folk lived much as they did on Peary Road. So let's travel to Winter Harbor Public Landing at the end of the road. Today we find a long dock with boats moored around the shore or near the end of the dock. One has access to a ramp to unload boats they've brought on trailers. A Marina operates in the area according to John Sanger. There is a parking lot with a small store for those, who fish for pleasure to purchase bait or snacks and drinks.

From April into November, each week a different locked vehicle sits in the parking area at the Public Landing day and night. The occupants go by boat across Winter Harbor to spend a quiet week at "The Hotel." I refer to a large two-story house that John Sanger's maternal grandparents, Claude and Hazel Parker, purchased land for after the "August Storm" in 1933. Sanger said the Parkers had learned that it was the only place the tide didn't cover in that hurricane. So they purchased the property.

The couple braved hauling building materials by boat and over the beach to construct the large structure. In time Parker's daughter, Irene Parker Sanger, lived in the house year around. Sanger taught in the Mathews Public School system. She had a four-wheel drive vehicle at the house, but preferred using the boat to travel to and from the Hotel when teaching. Winters weren't as fierce as in earlier years. Yet there were occasional snowstorms and biting winds when she crossed the span by boat.

The solid-wood-paneled walls in "The Hotel," as the location has been known in my 56 years in the area, give warmth to the house. The fireplaces are welcome to remove the chill of the evening in spring and fall. Sand on the beach around the shore sparkles in the sunshine. I visited The Hotel one evening in June 1968 for my son's graduation party, sponsored by our church. It intrigued me for the occasion or even a week in the summer, but not to live full time. A hammock, furnished by the owners, hung between two large shade trees. During a summer soon after that, our friends, Rev. and Mrs. George Robinson, who pastored a church in Richmond, Virginia, took their three children to The Hotel for a week. They visited me on their return before heading for home. I was anxious to know how they fared, knowing George would have enjoyed it. He had spent some childhood summers at his maternal grandmother's house in the Motorun area. Uncles or cousins saw he had experience fishing, clamming and crabbing. But his wife was an urban girl, originally from Ohio. Besides they might well have had their hands full, watching three urban children under 12 with water surrounding them. But she reported that she had one of the most relaxing and carefree weeks of her life. She had been able to read books evenings since the children fell to sleep early and easily. The entire family had enjoyed swimming and boating. Mrs. Robinson even raked clams one day since they were near shore. They had taken a good supply of food, but supplemented it with the catches of seafood from the surrounding waters. Her suntan told me she'd spent time out of doors. Should one wonder, The Hotel has water and sewage with one or more baths, electric lights with plugs for appliances and other modern conveniences. Sanger told me The Hotel is still in demand, booking well in advance.

The closed building where Peary Post Office last served nearby residents.

There was less demand for the full general-merchandise line after World War II since most patrons had automobiles to drive to town with larger self-service stores. William Armistead dismantled the original building, constructing a more modern store with a post office area. He stocked basic items and ordered nets, wire, anchors, oilskins, or whatever the watermen needed. Armistead remained postmaster until his unexpected death in 1979.

After William Armistead's service, Virginia Ann Shipley, Mary Ray and Harlene Pritchard served in Peary Post Office, the store having closed. In 1986, although the office served 46 families, the Post Office Officials saw the office as a liability. The cost to operate it amounted to $11,270 annually with income averaging $2,570. The postmaster recorded only four or five transactions a day, most under $3.

Patrons of Peary Post Office opted for various methods of delivery in absence of their office: 27 picked up their mail at locked boxed units in a cluster at the vicinity of the former post office delivered by the highway carrier; four rented lock boxes at Port Haywood; while the others chose Star Route delivery by the highway carrier to their homes. All mail went to Port Haywood. (Archives *Gloucester-Mathews Gazette-Journal*)

Today, P. Buckley Moss, an international artist, has moved her warehouse, known as "Moss Port Folio" to the county. But she and husband, Malcolm Henderson, enjoy her local studio and their home at the end of Peary Road. They have purchased two farmhouses, having belonged to the Pugh and Hall families in earlier years. From her second floor studio with many windows, she has a view of Horn Harbor, Winter Harbor or the Chesapeake Bay with the boats, wildlife and grasses. Some of her more recent paintings reflect water scenes.

Potato Neck remains a friendly community. Even though the general store and post office have closed, neighbors visit in their yards, around shore and on morning walks that make up for the store visits. There is a road, shown only on a new map as Shore Drive, which circles the shoreline that we enter by turning left near the end of Peary Road. Homes line the side facing the water. Perhaps they were meant to be summer homes, but many enjoy the view of the Harbor and Bay year around. Several have gardens, some large and others small, but farming is a thing of the past in Potato Neck.

Chapter Eight

*"A smile costs nothing, but gives much. It enriches those
who receive, without making poor those who give."*
The Richardson Review October 1927

Ruff Post Office Unique

Brooks Ruff, the only black to apply for a post office
in Mathews County, received his appointment in May 1910.
The office served 75 families at the time. Around the turn of
the century, Ruff had opened his general merchandise store
and shoe repair shop in the predominantly black community.
His wife, Mary Lola, assisted him in the post office. Ruff's
office stood in the corner of his store on Route 614,
Ridgefield Road. ("Black" was the appropriate term in the
time to which this refers.)

Customers at Ruff's store comprised a community of
small farms that fed the families. Only a few raised money
crops of beans and corn. Most of the men worked outside the
Ruff area on the water and for other residents, according to
an interview with Marion Smith by a *Gloucester-Mathews
Gazette Journal* reporter in 1982. Mr. Smith was a gardener,
not only at home but also for other residents of the county.

The blacks of the community attended Wayland
Baptist Church, which sat near Ruff's store. Meanwhile, the
white population attended Bethel Methodist Episcopal
Church at Laban. The first public school for the white
children was Beaverdam School while the blacks attended a
private school. Marion Smith related in her interview that
members of Wayland Baptist Church supported the school,
operating five months during the year. This private school

taught grades one through seven. It closed when Thomas Hunter opened in 1927, and the children walked there.

After Ruff died in the 1920s, Lola kept the store and post office operating for several years. But the community business had moved to a larger store and business district on Route 613, Beaverdam Road. Thus the post office service closed May 31, 1933, and Mrs. Ruff sold all the merchandise, closing the store. Mail went To Beaverlette Post Office.

Sarah Post Office

"How I wish I might travel all the way to your door for the pleasure of shaking your hand once more."
Post Card 1918

Edwin Hudgins had operated his store on route 609, Bethel Beach Road, for some years when he agreed with the community that they needed a post office nearer than Laban. The community had grown with residents building more homes down lanes to Winter Harbor, the southeast end of Ridgefield Road where it intersects Bethel Beach Road and on the main road passing his store, so he served sufficient people to justify the office. On his application, he knew no better name than Sarah, honoring his wife. After all, she would be doing most of the work. Wonder if he asked her permission.

Hudgins had the post office cage in place in the front corner of his store, ready for sending and delivering mail when his appointment came in February 1911. Edwin and Sarah Hudgins served the office until October 1933. At that time Randolph Hudgins and later his wife, Brazoria, served as postmasters until it closed in 1944. Mail went to Onemo Post Office.

Emmett Diggs lived near the end of Ridgefield Road towards Bethel Beach Road with his wife and two children,

Oliver and Dorothy. When old enough to walk a quarter mile alone, Dorothy enjoyed fetching the family's mail. She told me that she didn't want to go until she could get a fresh egg from the hen's nest. She'd take a round-tin bucket, which she also used for a lunch pail, with her egg in it to buy a piece of candy.

Evidentially, other children in the neighborhood did the same thing. A brother and sister, wishing to remain anonymous, walked together for the family's mail one day. They took two eggs to purchase their candy. Mr. Edwin Hudgins informed the siblings that he had some fine chocolate if they'd like to try it. They did, not knowing anything about Exlax®. By bedtime both children suffered with cramps and diarrhea. Upon questioning the children, the mother knew Hudgins had given them the new laxative, and she let Hudgins know what she thought of such an act. He'd chuckled earlier, but he knew better than to pull that stunt again.

After the contents had been sold, Edwin Hudgins' building was sold for a dwelling. The purchaser had to make proper modifications to convert it into an attractive home. Only those, who are old enough to remember today, know which building served the locals merchandise and provided mail service.

Sarah Post Office

Picture courtesy Carole Anne Diggs Hindman taken about 1965

Auburn Wharf Post Office

*"King George did not sign Magna Carta, as is so often
stated in school books and sometimes shown in pictures.
What he did was to affix his seal to the document.
He could not write his name."*
The Richardson Review October 1927

Although Dr. Henry Wythe Tabb had the training to
practice medicine in any city or hospital in the states, he
desired to come back to the Gloucester-Mathews area. First,
he wanted to marry the Mathews County girl, whom he had
loved and had seen too little of while studying. Second, he
preferred the country lifestyle that he'd known since birth to
the cities where he lived while preparing for the career he
desired. Thus his father, Phillip Tabb, began to build his
youngest son, Henry, a home. He chose 300 acres of the
1100 acre 1611 grant on North River in Mathews County.
(Dates and names taken from documents in the "Mathews
County Historical Society's" records, copied from infor-

mation Joseph Martin found in his research and the same has been stored in the State Archives: According to the documents, the estate was originally the property of the Mayo family. Edward Tabb, born February 3, 1719, was the son of John Tabb and Martha Mayo. She was a widow of a Mr. Hand at the time of her marriage to Tabb.)

Phillip Tabb had faith that Henry would develop the area much as Phillip's, own home at Toddsbury, and Henry's brothers Captain Phillip E. of Waverly Plantation and John of White Marsh Plantation.

Historical records do not fully agree as to when the house was started (most say 1820), but it wasn't completed until 1824 after Philip's death in 1822. Meanwhile, Dr. Henry Tabb had married Eliza (shown as Herietta and Hester in other documents) Van Bibber and lived in a smaller house on her father's property at Northend Plantation while they awaited the move to Auburn. But she died in childbirth in 1823, a year before the estate home had been completed. Henry's office sat in the yard at Auburn with his name and title in gold letters over the door. So he had begun his practice before or upon marrying Eliza.

The doctor moved and lived a lonely life at Auburn before he married his cousin, Martha Tabb Thompson of Popular Grove, in 1828. Meanwhile, Dr. Tabb had been establishing the other businesses on the estate; among them was a wharf for slopes to enter. However, no records verify one had been built before the Civil War. Among those Dr. Tabb had as his slaves was a carpenter, blacksmith, bricklayer, butcher and coachman. He treasured these slaves and would not sell either of them for $1,500 each. Records show that his 100 slaves were valued at $400 each, including the treasured ones. He hired an overseer, who had a home furnished him on the property. The doctor, with assistance of the overseer and slaves, farmed most of his land, raising cattle, sheep and hogs besides the many acres of corn, oats and wheat. He also hired a housekeeper, who had a room in the main house. She handled all the keys to closets, the cellars and storerooms.

Dr. Henry Tabb and Martha had five children, one son and four daughters before Martha died in 1842. Two of these children died in childhood, and Mary Eliza, spoken of in records as his beloved and eldest daughter, had a fatal accident in 1859.

In 1856, Dr. Tabb had married a classmate of Mary Eliza, Ellen Foster from Boston. Ellen was 30 years his junior. When Ellen's father visited Auburn, he wrote of a pleasant stay, relating many details. A quote reads, "The Doctor, I think, somewhat extravagant about his table. I told him one day, 'cooked enough for a regiment of soldiers.' This I suppose is owing to the frequent visits from one plantation to another... Then often we have but four at the table upon which you will find perhaps a round of beef, a roast of saddle mutton, a boiled ham, a beef steak and oysters cooked in a variety of ways. The dessert consists of pudding, pies, walnuts, almonds, grapes and (sometimes) oranges. Wine is then introduced and when one drinks his glass it is the signal for retiring."

Ellen Foster Tabb died the year before Mary Eliza's fatal fall--1858. Dr. Tabb lived until 1863, dying from a cancer that began on his face. The property remained in the family until 1896. After the Civil War, the plantation lands fell into disrepair. In the early 1900s, under new ownership, the lands were brought back to some of their original production. Shell Post Office sat near the wharf on the land owned by Auburn from 1899 to 1912. When Charles Heath, who owned the plantation, sold Auburn, Shell Post office closed.

In 1915 Mr. Robert F. Heitemeyer applied for a post office at Auburn Wharf. He received the appointment in April and served until February 1921. Robert Hicks verified the Heitemeyer family lived at Auburn during this time in an interview. When it closed, mail went to Cardinal. Though little reference is made to the post office, merchants from the general merchandise stores in the area tell of receiving shipments at the wharf regularly. They included merchants at North Post Office, and Cardinal Post Office. I also have found reference to "drummers" coming to Auburn Wharf on the steamboat and a few passengers after 1921. (Much of the information regarding Auburn in "Mathews County Historical Society" Records with authentication.)

Beaverlette Post Office

""A gentleman who was asked for his marriage certificate,
quietly took off his hat and
pointed to a bald spot on his head."
The Richardson Review September 1927

When activities at Ruff's store, where he had his post office, slowed, "things were going in full swing down at Beaverlette," according to Gilmour Diggs in a 1982 interview with a *Gloucester-Mathews Gazette Journal* reporter.

Near the corner of Route 613, Beaverdam Road, and Route 614, Ridgefield Road, Cecil Oscar Hudgins owned a general merchandise store. Garden Creek flowed as far as Beaverlette area described in the days our forefathers settled the area. Though it had become no more than a large ditch, beavers had built a dam across it—thus the name Beaverdam. Hudgins' son, W.E. Hudgins, better known as "Ed," felt they needed a post office even though Ruff Post Office sat less than half a mile up the road. He applied, requesting the name Beaverdam, but was denied the name since one exited by that name in Hanover County. His appointment came, showing the post office named Beaverlette in October 1916.

It is evident that Ed Hudgins had an assistant to stay in the post office. He developed a series of businesses in several buildings beyond the store. One housed the planning mill with lumber piled on the side. Hudgins purchased the lumber from a sawmill in Dutton and hauled it on a Model T Ford truck. When his older son, Cecil, became old enough, he and employees used the dressed boards to fill orders. They built truck bodies, school buses, boats and furniture in another section of the large building.

W. E. Hudgins & Son's business became quite familiar to me because my husband, Kirby, apprenticed under Mr. Ed and Cecil, as a cabinetmaker, in the late 1940s after World War II. However, cabinet making at Mr. Ed's included not only cabinets of all kinds, but also the items mentioned above, restoring furniture and an occasional upholstery job. In fact, after Kirby purchased his first truck, a bright yellow Studerbaker, for our business, "The Craftsman Shop", he built the body in his own shop like Hudgins had taught him. I sewed my first upholstery on my home machine for the business at Beaverlette since Mr. Ed's wife was deceased and Cecil's wife ill. I used the money that I earned to help pay for a crib for our first child—a son, Wade Kirkwood.

I'll never forget the queer feeling I got in my stomach when I took an unusual handle for a scraper to Pleasant's Hardware in Richmond, Virginia, to purchase blades for it. The store sat on Broad Street. Kirby had died the previous year, and I had the responsibility of seeing his work completed, as well as, managing the retail business that I operated in Mathews Court House. A salesman had greeted me with, "And what may I do for you?" I pulled the scraper handle from a paper sack, telling the man I needed six blades for it. "Oh! You are from Mathews County," he exclaimed. I inquired how'd he know. "Well, I never saw a scraper like that anywhere except Ed Hudgins' boat building shop." Still puzzled, I said that I expected it had come from Mr. Ed's shop since my husband had worked for Mr. Ed. Then when Cecil closed the business, Kirby purchased many of the hand tools. "Well, it's a small world. Ed Hudgins designed that devise to fit these blades," and he pulled out the six that I needed.

There was a gristmill, powered by a gasoline engine in another building. The late Gilmour Diggs mentioned the corner became quite busy late Fridays or Saturdays. Wagons and a few buggies sat in line, waiting their turn to have corn ground for the Sunday's batter bread and the following week's cooking.

Brothers, Harry Hudgins and Harvey Hudgins, built boats in their private yards. Harry and Harvey were my daddy's step uncles so we often visited them with Grandpa and his second wife, Granny Callis, on Sunday afternoons. Grandmother Callis had died when daddy was in his tenth year. So as a child, I saw the Hudgins' brothers' boat building operations often. Neither brother had a building in which to work. They stored their tools in buildings in their back yards, living across the road from each other.

The corner also had a wheelwright shop. In another shop, Mr. Will Owens worked for Lester and Marvin Hudgins, repairing automobiles after they came on the scene.

The post office sat in the corner of Ed's father, Oscar Hudgins' store, adjoining the land of the other Hudgins' buildings in later years. Both whites and blacks had met at Ruff's store when fetching mail. However, with the Hudgins' store open, they became as segregated as the schools and churches, with the white men gathering in Oscar Hudgins' store every evening except Sundays. No business except an eating establishment opened on Sunday in Mathews County until late in the twentieth century. Gilmour Diggs' said men stayed at his great grandfather's store until midnight, playing cards. "We made sandwiches or whatever and had a ball," he remembered.

Brooke C. Ripley, who started teaching the white children at Beaverdam School in 1928, told the *Gloucester-Mathews Gazette-Journal* reporter in 1982 that during the "big" recess" (noon to 1:00 p.m.), a boy would travel up to Ruff to gather the mail for Beaverlette. In it's early years, Beaverdam School taught grades one through high school. However by 1928, it only taught through grade seven. Then with the consolidation of schools, they taught only three grades until it closed in 1939.

Mrs. Ripley spoke of her years at Beverdam School with fond memories. She told that parents were more involved with their children's education and the operation of the school. Men kept the woodshed supplied for winter months. She assigned such jobs as getting water from a neighbor's well and tending the fire to the children. The school provided a shed for the children, who rode ponies to school, to keep them. When the weather was too bad to play outside, Mrs. Ripley cut recesses short and let the children go home early. She remembered how hard the residents tried to keep the school when consolidation came, but they had to accept the more practical.

Brooke Ripley's husband worked as an engineer on a tugboat that hauled oil. Gilmour Diggs' father painted houses; while others in the neighborhood sailed longer distances than those on tugboats. When work became available across the York River, fewer left home for long stays. All had one or more cows, horses and fowl besides raising a garden and feed for the animals.

Mr. Rudolph Small, of Beaverlette, where I visited often before and soon after my early school years, had a small but unique family farm. Daddy's stepbrother, James Owens, had married Louise Small. Since Rudolph's wife was deceased, he offered Louise and James a home if they'd stay with him and his younger sons. James worked on ships, being gone for long periods. But when he came home, we visited the family with Grandpa and Granny Callis. Aunt Louise and Momma both enjoyed cooking and sewing. They bonded. So when Uncle James died April 1932 at age 29, Momma and Daddy bundled my sister and me up and went to the house to stay overnight. In those days, the bodies were brought to the house. But a group of family and neighbors sat to guard it by night. Momma and we girls, not only spent the night, but also stayed until after the funeral. I began to marvel at the things Mr. Small grew in his garden. He brought homegrown celery in the house among other things. Even the leaves had bleached white while under the soil for protection against the cold. Aunt Louise was carrying the couple's second child and needed Momma's help. That was just the beginning of visits. We were at the house on the morning of February 2nd—Ground Hog's Day 1933, having spent the night. And Mr. Small had a ground hog in a mounded hill that he'd made of soil. He and his two sons arose early to see if the ground hog saw his shadow. I watched from the window as he scooted back into the hill. Aunt Louise and her girls spent many days at our house, giving her a chance to sew for the three of them before she moved to Baltimore to work.

With time, Joseph Edward Sadler, known as "Ed Sadler," had built a new store for general merchandise with a shed room on the side for a warehouse. He operated as J.E. Sadler & Co. As Oscar Hudgins grew older, he closed his store. So W. Edward Hudgins moved the post office to Sadler's store. Since Hudgins only took care of the business end of his office, the move was good, keeping the post office across the road from its original location. Hudgins could gather with the other men in the evening to catch up on any news he hadn't heard. Ed Hudgins retired from the post office in January 1949, and his son Cecil accepted the job until June of that year. Virginia Hudgins was appointed June 9, 1949, and served while keeping basics in the store until 1972. Mildred Sadler became the official postmaster, serving 14 years in both post office and storekeeper before her retirement. When Sadler retired, the merchandise was discontinued. Officers in Charge took over until the office closed in the early 1990s. Mary Lee Fernald was the last OIC to serve. She worked as long as physical body, which battled cancer, allowed her to serve the patrons that she'd learn to love. Most patrons have highway carrier delivery at their homes today.

Beaverlette Post Office sat in the corner of Ed Sadler's store.

Onemo becomes One Mo' Post Office

> *"Parson to boy: '*
> *Do you know where little boys go to that smoke?'*
>
> *Boy to parson:*
> *'Down behind the shed, sir!'"*
> Post Card 1916

On a Saturday morning in late spring of 1919, Richard J. Brooks, known as Dick Brooks, unhitched his horse from the cart, tying her to graze in the field on the side of Route 609, Bethel Beach Road. Then he gathered the mail for the store, Norfolk's Virginia Pilot newspapers, wife Annie's letter from Baltimore, and the neighbors' mail from the cart. Stomping his feet clean at the door, Brooks strolled into his general-merchandise store. He dumped the pile of mail on the counter.

"We surely need another post office closer than Laban," Brooks said to no one in particular. Besides his wife Annie, Thomas Rufus Weston, who taught school and Victor Hudgins heard the remark since the two regulars warmed themselves on nail kegs around the stove.

"I told you that a year ago," neighbor Victor Hudgins replied.

"Annie, write a letter to the Post Office Department to that address 'Charlie Anthony' gave me," Brooks chided.

"What you goin' to name it?" Hudgins queried.

"Let's call it 'one more,'" Weston said.

"It's just one mo' post office on the side of the road." Dick Brooks agreed. "But I know if they want signatures, the Unk Brooks clan will furnish plenty. We're less than two miles from Garden Creek, where their houses sit, but it's six miles to Laban Post Office if they take all the short cuts from where Kirby and Bathesheba live."

"One Mo," Hudgins said. "Why not ask for that."

Since Brooks had counted over 200 people with the children in the area on Winter Harbor, continuing to Garden Creek, he felt he'd have no problem obtaining his office.

When the acceptance came, dated October 20, 1919, the department had assigned "Onemo" as the official name (pronounced Oh-nee-mo' today). Richard J. Brooks received appointment as postmaster. But we know from family members that Annie did most of the post office work. Twenty-one years later, circumstances required that Dick and Annie close their store, and Onemo Post Office closed for a time on December 21, 1940. (Information given by Edith Brooks and Elwood Kirby Brooks, Sr., my in-laws, and confirmed by Victor Hudgins and USPS records.)

Some of the more prominent men in the northern Winter Harbor area made their living on the water, selling oysters or fishing nets. There was always a ready market for fish. Earlier, Victor's father, John Wesley Hudgins, had operated a bugeye—a two masted sailing vessel—going from Winter Harbor to Norfolk on a weekly basis. That was before the Norfolk Steamboat's run. The vessel would carry whatever products people in the area had to sell, and sometimes return with a passenger. He ran the bugeye for 17 years. (*Gloucester-Mathews Gazette Journal* April 20, 1989)

Victor Hudgins would talk about "way back in olden times when a lot of sailing vessels were built in this county." His father's bugeye had been built at Laban, the nearest post office to Onemo. Rev. Wilbur C. Diggs, who was my husband's grandfather, gave Kirby and me a deed to the plot of land that had been a canoe yard. We built our home and business, "The Craftsman Shop," on the property in the late 1940s and early 50s. The road that circles from Bethel Beach Road to Garden Creek Road, in front of our former place, has been named "Canoe Yard Trail."

Aubrey Morgan, another lifetime resident in the Onemo area, served on the Board Of Supervisors of Mathews County and lived next door to our house. He told about children's education in the community. Woodland School had once sat near Laban Post Office before Winter Harbor School appeared. Woodland consolidated into Winter Harbor School. The latter three-room school taught grades 1-7 when Morgan was a scholar. When completing the seventh grade, one went to New Point School if they went on through high school. Meanwhile, Eunice Brooks, who lived on Route 609, Bethel Beach Road, down towards the beach, taught a private school in her home.

Most families had a "provision farm" to feed their families, according to Victor Hudgins in the *Gloucester-Mathews Gazette-Journal* article. The Diggs' family had the largest farm in the community. Monroe Diggs, known as "Mon," had 40-45 acres where he raised grain for livestock. James Brooks' property, where his sons George Enos and Grayson lived, had less acreage, but they raised cattle and other farm animals, plus garden vegetables and feed for the animals. George Enos also oystered, and in time became "Oyster Inspector," working for Virginia Marine Resources. He knew every piece of oyster shore, the owners and boundaries, appearing in Richmond when he was needed in a dispute. In the 1970s, the *Richmond Times Dispatch* published an article about his remarkable memory, concerning the properties, after one of the sessions there.

Charlie T. Diggs, known as "Charlie Mon," had sent his application to the Assistant Postmaster General in Washington D.C. before Dick and Annie closed their store, requesting permission to move the office up the road to Charlie Brooks' large general-merchandise store. Diggs would serve as postmaster. Approval came on January 8, 1941, a matter of days after the Brooks closing. Diggs served as postmaster until 1955 except for his two terms of service in the U.S. Navy—World War II in the Pacific and during the Korean War for one year in Germany. Mary Stewart, his assistant, accepted appointment for those terms and my husband was her assistant during the Korean War. Before 1950, the post office moved nearer Laban for a time, but folks had automobiles and didn't mind. At that time, Diggs had moved the post office to his own store on the corner of Bethel Beach Road and Garden Creek Road.

When Charlie Diggs retired in 1955, the office moved back to the store that Charlie Brooks had owned. Charlie Downs had purchased the general-merchandise store, joining in a partnership with his son, Jennings. Alma Downs, Jennings' wife, applied for the postmaster's position, knowing Diggs planned to retire. She received appointment September 1958, serving until Jennings had decided to sell out the general-merchandise business. He'd decided to work with his brother in his store in Maryland, and Alma was able to obtain a post office job in that area. The old store was hard to heat due to its size and had no water. So without a store, there needed to be a change.

Lowery and Glenna Hudgins built a small post office on the corner of their property, a short distance from the Downs' store that Charlie Brooks had built many years earlier. Glenna served as the first postmaster in the new building. When I interviewed the postmaster in 2004, Debbie

Richardson served as postmaster with approximately 110 post office boxes in use and a number of highway carrier Star Route deliveries.

People with other names now own the Brooks' properties in the area Unk Brooks' descendents lived. They have moved into area in the mid and latter part of the twentieth century. The last Brooks' home in that vicinity burnt due to an electrical defect after it had been sold and was being reconstructed. A better part of the land that made up that, the James Brooks' farm, has been donated to the Wetlands Commission. Edward Kirby Brooks,' my husband's grandfather's, house had burnt earlier during a cold freeze. The couple, who had purchased the house only months earlier, tried to keep their pipes from freezing, losing everything in the fire the heater started. They escaped with little of anything, but their lives.

Picture courtesy Virginia Downs Adams

Onemo Post Office served from this store twice.

The front right hand corner of the store Charles Brooks built and kept until he retired. Charlie W. Downs

purchased the property and continued the general merchandise business with his son Jennings joining in partnership after he completed high school. The dark color looked liked many stores and warehouses in my childhood. Linseed oil and umber preserved the wood and gave the dark brown color.

Another incident that drew the press's attention occurred in 2003 to an Onemo patron. After the highway carrier delivered Pauline Diggs' mail in early August 2003, she opened a Christmas greeting. She decided her nephew and his wife were ahead of schedule this year. But as Mrs. Diggs began to read the hand written message, she realized she had already attended the affairs about which they wrote. So she pulled the envelope from the trashcan, learning it had left West Virginia on December 23, 2002. Then she found a second postmark that read Richmond, VA, July 15, 2003. Wonder where it lay during those months?

Monica Harris lives on a piece of the property, which one of the Brooks families had owned until the 1930s or later. I saw her soon after Powell Hudgins, a lifetime resident near Winter Harbor, had died in the spring of 2003. She suggested that I read her article in "Readers Write" section of the *Gloucester-Mathews Gazette Journal,* referring to Onemo Post Office.

Harris is a well-educated woman, and I respect her comments. She had told one of her daughters that Powell had died and was surprised at her reaction. The daughter hadn't lived here in years and had only known him through brief encounters at the post office. But she was genuinely sad and added, "He was a real character and a really good man. What better epitaph could a person hope for?"

"Many days Powell set the tone for my day," Harris continued. "If I ran into him at the Post Office he always made me smile if not laugh out loud at his outrageous tall tales. He was always a day brightener for everyone he encountered and he encountered lots of people in his days. He was the Energizer Bunny of good cheer—he never had a down day.

"Powell loved Mathews County. His passing caused me to reflect on why we chose to live in Mathews—which was not our plan but a decision we never regretted. We came here 18 years ago as 'summer come-heres' and complications in building our house in such a remote area forced us to stay here for a year. When six of us moved from a fairly large 11-room house into a one-bedroom 1950s vintage trailer all our friends thought we had lost our minds, (Some still do.) But it was people like Powell and Aubrey Morgan, Mable Sadler and Victor Hudgins who motivated us to stay.

"We could have settled in a nice homogeneous neighborhood in suburbia where prestige, perfect lawns, and big houses were important. But what kind of values would that impart to our children?

"We are blessed to know older people and wiser people. Poor people who live next door to rich people (and who knows or cares about the difference)? We love living with neighbors who can see and enjoy God's work in daffodils even in an unmowed lawn. At Powell's funeral one of his daughters spoke about how he dressed down but didn't care because people who knew him knew he could dress better if he wanted and those who didn't—didn't matter. Those are the values that make Mathews the special place that it is.

"Powell was the last of the old timers our children grew up with. I didn't realize until recently how they had influenced our lives and our values. They weren't preachy or self-righteous and probably had no idea that their genuine kindness and goodness made them role models but I'm sure that they were. I hope that those of us who were touched by these fine people will be worthy to carry on their legacy so

175

we can retain the special place we have in Mathews County."
Signed, Monica Harris

Shadow Post Office Established South of Susan

*"If we had paid no more attention to our plants
than we have to our children, we would now be living in a
jungle of weeds."*
Luther Burbank—*The Richardson Review* February 1927

Roland M. Hudgins spent a good bit of his childhood
with his father, Milton Hudgins, in his general-merchandise
store. Having worked in the store since he was old enough to
count, Roland joined his father in partnership for a time. But
later, Roland purchased John T. White's store, operating on
his own. The store Roland purchased sat near New Point
School. Roland's wife made 2½-gallon freezers of ice cream,
selling cones for 5 cents each. A scope of ice cream was a
full cup in those days so one cone was aplenty. The school
children were allowed to walk to Hudgins' store and buy ice
cream cones at "big" recess, which was 12:00 noon to 1:00
p.m. If for some reason, they missed out at lunchtime, they
could go by the store on their way home for their cones. One
couldn't purchase cartons of ice cream for home use until
some years later so it was always a treat.

It was evenings in 1921, when Roland Hudgins and
his customers determined it was time for them to have a post
office. Susan Post Office sat up the road and Motorun Post
office way down near Bayside Wharf. Roland M. Hudgins
general merchandise store had become their regular meeting
place. So when Roland or his wife picked up the store's mail,
they got many of his neighbors' newspapers and letters,
bringing them to the store near New Point School.

When Hudgins applied to the Assistant Postmaster
General in Washington, D.C. for his office to serve the 150
people living within walking distance of the store, he

requested the name "Harbor" or "Nash." Both names were denied, but they accepted "Shadow," Roland Hudgins' nickname. Wonder who suggested the name? Perhaps in his first request, he was thinking of nearby Horn Harbor, but no one knows why he thought of "Nash" unless he drove a Nash automobile, which had first come on the market in 1916. Roland's store burnt about 1926.

Charles R. Brooks had a store across the road from the Hudgins store. Charles' father, John C. Brooks, had built the store. Like their competitor, the son had worked with his father as a youth, forming a partnership, known as Brooks & Son when he became older. It seems obvious that Brooks had accepted the mail delivery to his store after the fire since the National Archives don't show a delay in mail delivery to the office. The only other factual thing we do know is that Charles Brooks became postmaster in April 1926. He managed the store while his wife, the former Lottie Morgan from the Diggs community, served in the post office. They served the post office for 33 years.

Before Brooks retired, Nancy H. Hudgins had someone build a "shadow" of a place for the post office across from the school. A *Gloucester-Mathews Gazette Journal* reporter said that Hudgins wanted it large enough for two or three customers to gather. The Assistant Postmaster General appointed Mrs. Hudgins as postmaster October 1, 1959. One record stated Mrs. Hudgins bristled at the suggestion only she, the rural mail carrier and one customer could get in the building. On a summer's day, one found a bench, two chairs with well-worn cushions and a fan in the building. Customers could still stand. Mrs. Hudgins said that in the Christmas rush, as many as 12 people crowded in the building. "They got cluttered together, mailing letters, packages and cards," she said. Mrs. Hudgins opened mornings at 11:30, closing at 3:30 in the afternoon. At times it was a busy four hours.

Mrs. Hudgins wrote money orders for two older sickly sisters and delivered or mailed them. A request for the unique address caught the eye of many cancellation collectors. They would send prepaid post cards in an envelope from as far away as Arizona, requesting the postmaster write a message from Shadow. She would write that she remembered days when the mail arrived on the steamboat from Norfolk. She never took the time to write the cards until she had mail call for the day completed and the mail ready for the 2:30 pick up.

The residents at Shadow while Mrs. Hudgins served as postmaster either worked across the river or on the water. Beulah United Methodist Church sat near Motorun and St. Paul United Methodist Church was near Susan. But though the residents attended the local churches or others in the county during the early years, New Point School took central position in the Shadow community. The residents supported the school building where students in grades one through high school attended. When it needed repair or they had a special project, the principal never had to go to the school board for help. The Community Civic League saw that the school raised the funds with school plays or other fundraisers. After the plays, the women often auctioned homemade cakes to add to the money raised. Dinners, hot dog sandwiches and ice cream cones served at May Day brought even more for the project that was in progress. Parents and relatives worked together, creating a close-knit community.

Nancy H. Hudgins retired September 30, 1988, and Shadow Post office closed. The mail went to Susan Post office.

"That mansion belongs to the richest man in New York. He has a German cook, a French maid, a Jap valet, an Irish chauffer, a Scotch garage mechanic, Swedish housekeeper and an American secretary." "That ain't a mansion. That's a world court." "Selected" *The Richardson Review* October 1927

Shadow Post Office sat in the corner of Charles R. Brooks Store 33 years after its installation in 1926. He was postmaster, but his wife, Lottie Morgan Brooks, did the post office work during the day and her husband at night. When the store closed, the post office moved across the road to the "shadow" of a building.

Chapter Nine

"Did you know, you forgot to Write,
Alright, What's Wrong?" Haint your ink well?
Post Card 1912, featuring Daffydils' Comic)

Miles Store Post Office on North River Road

In the booming 1920s when Calvin Coolidge was president, Carroll H. Miles, Sr., known as "Eddie" Miles, built a general-merchandise store. He ordered the building, which sat on East River Road opposite the end of Hicks Wharf Road, have columns in front to give it architectural style. Even though Hicks Wharf Post Office was still open in 1929, Miles applied for an office to serve the folks who lived down the other roads and lanes near his store. They purchased groceries and supplies at Miles Store so they'd like to fetch their mail on the same trip. Miles, who received a prompt reply, received his appointment as postmaster of Miles Store Post Office in June 1929. His wife, Grace Elizabeth, known as "Gracie," assisted Eddie in the post office. (Information from *Gloucester-Mathews Gazette-Journal*)

When Hicks Wharf Post Office closed in 1937, their mail went to Miles Store, increasing their patrons. Eddie Miles was the official postmaster until April 1942 when Grace became the temporary postmaster. She received her appointment on June 6th of the same year. During Grace's term in 1950, the Post Office Department changed Miles Store P.O. to Miles Post Office. She served until the end of April 1957 when her daughter Evelyn, who served as her assistant, became the official postmaster.

It was after the post office had been established that Eddie Miles built his corrugated metal building with a flat roof. The building served as an office and warehouse for his feed business, according to Kenneth Jordan, Jr. At a later date, Kenneth Hugh Jordan, Sr. purchased the feed business and operated a wholesale feed and seed business from the building.

When Evelyn Miles retired in October 1960, the post office moved to Jordan's building. Whether the Miles family had at any time use of the same post office cage, some call "window," from Hicks Wharf Post Office is uncertain. But when Mary F. Jordan moved the office to the corner of Jordan's feed and seed business, she installed the cage from Hicks Wharf P.O. Mary became the official postmaster October 20, 1960, serving 18 years. Upon her retirement, Sue Kilmon served until the office closed at the end of December 1987.

Sue Kilmon had told a *Gloucester-Mathews Gazette Journal* reporter in August 1983 that she had a post office that is "small, old and in need of repair in many ways." The article explained that it was in the corner of an otherwise vacant building with uninsulated walls and corrugated metal siding. The post office opened four hours a day, serving only 70 families. It had no boxes for rent, no bathroom, no window screens and just one small space heater. At that date, the postal service was looking for new land on which to erect a modern office. Money had been allocated for updating post offices at the time. It's evident they didn't find land since nothing materialized. In a news release in December 1987, the *Gloucester-Mathews Gazette Journal* announced the closing of Miles Post Office in bold headlines. Customers would receive mail, except for one family, at Cardinal, where Kilmon had already been appointed after Nancy Small's death earlier in the year. Although the patrons had increased to 100 families, a new building site or improvements to the old building had not materialized. Kilmon's load increased when she began work at Cardinal Post Office. The merging of the two post offices made 300 families to serve.

Miles Post Office

Pribble Post Office

"New Year's Greeting"

"I'd like to be with you today,
To say to you "All hail,"
But as I am too far away,
I'll say it still by mail.

(Post card sent by admirer to Irene Brooks 1911)

We refer to White's Neck from time to time. Where is this place? When one leaves either Foster or North Post Office, turning down either East River or North River Road, they are near White's Neck. It's the entire peninsula, ending at the point where East River and North River meet the Mobjack Bay—the largest of the necks in Mathews County. Tick Neck, the smaller neck, forks off East River Road, beginning a bit south of Foster's Post Office.

In the 1920s, when business boomed in the United States, Golly Borum built a small general-merchandise store at the corner of Turnpike and North River Roads. Turnpike Road "wasn't much more than a mud puddle," according to Mrs. Holland White in an interview with the *Gloucester-Mathews Gazette Journal* reporter in 1983. Turnpike Road hadn't always exited, but it became a necessity with progress. When black children needed to go from North River Road to Hicks Wharf School, there had been trees and underbrush in the way. In turn the white teachers and students, traveling to the Peninsula School met with the same problem. So the men felled trees between the two, making a road. Remember in those days, people either walked or traveled by horse or horse and buggy so a short route was imperative.

Referring to Borum's general-merchandise store, Lindsay Hudgins, a lifetime resident, told the reporter: "Mail, hardware, dry goods and other items would have to be picked up in Bohannon." So it is evident that people received mail at the store before an office was established. Bohannon

183

sat on the east end of Turnpike Road.

Borum found need to put his store on the market in late 1920s. Mr. and Mrs. Edwin Griffis purchased the property, reopening the general-merchandise store. Lucy R. Griffis, Edwin's wife, applied for a post office, suggesting the name "Pike." Mrs. Holland White was sister of Mrs. Griffis and gave the Gloucester-Mathews *Gazette Journal* reporter this information. When Griffis appointment came, the office of Assistant Postmaster General in Washington, D.C. had scratched "Pike and penned in "Pribble." Evidently, it was given as a second choice since I have found some gave two or more choices. Mr. Pribble, a Methodist minister, who had married another sister of the new postmaster, had a large farm in the neighborhood.

The Griffis no longer had to travel to Bohannon to bring the mail to the small building after April 1929. Pribble Post Office had been made official with daily deliveries. The men, who didn't farm or harvest the Rivers and Bays or go to sea on freight ships, worked on the other side of York River in the mid 1930s and beyond. Some traveled to work in Norfolk at the New York, Philadelphia and Norfolk Railroad. Others worked in the Newport News Shipyard, at Naval Weapons Station, Langley Field or other government facilities. Part of these workers came home every night; others on weekends and some worked two weeks on and one or two off. With money available for more automobiles, the smaller stores suffered loss in trade. By 1941, Edwin Griffis only cleared $15 on a Saturday night, which had been the high point of the business week in his store during earlier years. The post office closed on June 19th of that year. Edwin Griffis had obtained work in Newport News Shipyard, moving his family there after the store closed.

The building, where the post office had operated, sold, becoming a dwelling. Mail went to Bohannon. With better roads and easier transportation, no one missed the post office, as they would have sooner.

Bavon Post Office Sat on Corner

"Merry Christmas"

"You may hear it in the parlor,
Or hear it on the street
But when you see it on my greeting,
You know it's hard to beat."

1923 Post card to Irene Brooks from a student

The corner where Route 14, New Point Comfort Highway, ends, it meets Route 600. It now becomes Circle Drive to the right and Lighthouse Road to the left. It had been an ideal place for a store and post office when Motorun sat there according to residents on down near New Point Beach and Bayside Wharf. But new postmasters moved Motorun Post Office to the western end of Circle Drive and later farther down the Drive towards Shadow. The residents, who had established this office, felt it inconvenient.

Richard Burroughs solved the problem when he built and stocked his own general-merchandise store in 1935. It sat on the site where Motorun had first been located, facing Circle Drive. Burroughs and the neighbors wanted their own mail delivery. So he sent his application to the Assistant Postmaster General in Washington, D.C., but in his father's name, Walter Burroughs, since he was only 20 years old at that date—21 was the legal age for a postmaster. Richard and his wife had rooms for living in the back of the store when it first opened, according to my conversation with Marion Gray Burroughs Trusch, who has lived across from the store and post office through the years.

Burroughs received acceptance for the office June 1935. He had given several names from which the Assistant Post Office General's Office could choose, suggesting "Burroughs" as his first choice. However, they accepted Bavon, naming it for the beach beyond Lighthouse Road.

Some folk think I'm talking about the end of the county when I mention Bavon. In fact, Charlotte Crist wrote a most interesting article for the *Gloucester-Mathews Gazette Journal* in 1988, from which I quote. "When people try to go 'through' instead of 'to' Mathews County, they most likely end up at Bavon where Rt. 14 will deliver them within a stone's throw of Mobjack Bay."

Should one turn left on Lighthouse Road at Bavon, they find both older and modern homes. Lighthouse Road takes one by the road leading to the former Bayside Wharf, but Route 600 continues to the public dock and New Point Lighthouse Observatory. To the left the road leads a bit farther to a fork. One sign, reading "Private" and another that says "Chesapeake Shores," where Bavon Beach, which I knew as New Point Beach in the early 1940s, lays on the shore beyond the row of homes—some small and others large contemporary dwellings line the water's edge. It hasn't always been like that. Quoting the *Gloucester-Mathews Gazette Journal*: "Prior to World War II, the beach was primarily owned by George Pritchett and Coles Thomas, who were generous about public access to the beach." My church had several Sunday School picnics on the beach during the pre- war period.

In the spring of 1943, the U.S. Army leased the land from Pritchett and Thomas to establish an anti-aircraft training camp. Evelyn Pritchett remembered when the Army built barracks on concrete slabs, garages, a chow hall, a post exchange and an incinerator on the land that her father-in-law had been farming she told a *Gloucester-Mathews Gazette Journal* reporter in 1988. "A permanent company of approximately 100 men lived at the camp and trained a steady stream of soldiers brought in from Fort Eustis," Mrs. Pritchett said.

"They practiced shooting down a target that was towed behind an airplane," she said. "The firing made an awful lot of noise."

According to Mrs. Pritchett, they were good neighbors, treating children, who accompanied their parents to the camp, with hands full of candy. They only stayed a year, selling or dismantling the buildings. The concrete slabs remained for years.

Following the war, the land that supported the Army camp was sold to developers, resulting in a beach divided into lots for the homes to which I referred.

Returning to the history of the famed New Point Comfort Lighthouse, I learn that when they built the structure, the island had contained approximately 100 acres plus a narrow strip of land connecting it to the mainland. In an interview with the late Thomas Gayle, whose maternal grandparents, Mr. And Mrs. Wesley Ripley, lived on the island during his childhood, he gave the *Gloucester-Mathews Gazette Journal* reporter a description of the island during the first quarter of the twentieth century. The two-story dwelling that sat near the lighthouse had a kitchen with a water pump, dining room, sitting room and three bedrooms. Gayle remembered a porch swing, which takes me back to my childhood when relaxing in a porch swing became an enjoyable pastime. But there had also been a hotel in earlier years, a bathhouse, and a building where they sold drinks and sandwiches. Crowds came by boat during the summer to swim and picnic on the island. A large dock served the watermen, especially the fishermen. (Gayle didn't remember the hotel so it had met catastrophe in the late 1800s or early 1900s.)

"They would come in with their catch, and it would be boxed and iced, ready for loading aboard the steamer," Gayle said about the fisherman. "There was always a canning factory out there that processed salt herring. There were several large buildings and it employed about 25-30 people."

Lighting the lighthouse was a ritual that Gayle said had to be accomplished three times daily. "The keeper climbed the circular stairs to the glassed in top of the 100 ft. tower to light the lamp at sunset, then to change it at midnight, and to turn it out at sunrise.

"It was a kerosene lamp set in a keg of shaped prism so that the reflection could be seen farther," Gayle continued. "He recalled that boardwalks were laid between the dwelling and lighthouse, and around to a cellar, stable, and a storage shed."

I had learned the fierce 1933 August hurricane had cut the peninsula into, leaving the lighthouse on an island, I phoned Mrs. Marion Grey Trusch as to the route one took to reach New Point Comfort in that period. They went by boat from New Point Beach, now Chesapeake Shores or Bavon Beach. Trusch remembered that some of the older boys rolled up their trouser legs and waded across in summer to play or visit the lighthouse keeper. Now it's only accessible by boat, storms having completely isolated the lighthouse.

High winds and forcing waters has sliced the land away. What the 1933 hurricane didn't destroy, other nor'easters and hurricanes have played havoc, destroying all buildings except the lighthouse. A reef of rocks surrounds the lighthouse, but repairs are needed after these storms on a regular basis. Citizens have installed a new light in the tower during the past decade, adding to the charm of the prized lighthouse.

I mentioned passing the road to Bayside Wharf, where Route 14 picks up again. It has become Old Bayside Drive. The wharf boasted a motorized car that traveled down the half-mile long wharf on tracks to deliver merchandise and ice to steamers and boats. Hilton Greene operated an ice plant at Bayside as well as the wharf. The 1933 storm completely washed the pier away, but Greene rebuilt it to have it torn down the second time by Hurricane Hazel in 1954. Fires destroyed any parts of the pier and warehouses left. However, the large building where Greene stored ice is now a private home. On a drive to the end of Route 14, with a friend since I've been researching and writing this book, I recognized only two homes.

Returning to Bavon Post Office, in April 1944 Charles D. Hutson purchased the store, becoming the new postmaster. His wife, the former Mary Virginia Gayle, assisted him in the busy hours. Hutson died unexpectedly in 1945. So Mary Virginia Hutson became the official postmaster in November 1946, serving until about 1958. Bavon, like the other country stores, had become a neighborhood-gathering place. To learn about the illness, births, deaths and even world news the women went to the store after the mail truck had come during the day and the men "chewed fat," according to Hutson's daughter, Mrs. Joyce Hutson Hudgins, in the evenings. It remained a store until Mrs. Hutson's last days of service in the late 1950s. Mrs. Joyce Hudgins qualified as an assistant postmaster and served the office when needed.

Upon Hutson's retirement, Alma Downs became the postmaster. When Downs moved to another post office, officers in charge acted as postmaster. The *Gloucester-Mathews Gazette Journal* published an article about Bavon in May of 1985 when Helen Hurst was the OIC. Hurst told that the Class C office stayed open four hours a day, six days week.

The reporter, telling about how times had changed the community, said the huge docks on Davis Creek tell of a time when boats were larger and more plentiful. Docks lined the three-pronged creek. Mrs. Archie Hutson, who purchased seafood to sell, noted that Calvin Haywood and Lemuel Brown were probably the only fishermen, who still put out nets in the area in 1985. Buyers were almost stacked on top of each other, but Mrs. Hutson said they had "to stay in cahoots" with a mischievous look. She continued to tell she'd lived in the community for 49 years and once knew everyone. But she only knew 10-12 families at that date.

Strangers had moved into the houses when local residents moved or died.

It was in an interview this reporter had with Mrs. Trusch's mother, Mrs. Norman Burroughs, who told about attending a small private school before New Point School was built in 1911. The one-room schoolhouse held 20-25 pupils with Nellie Thomas teaching all grades. The school on Route 14 didn't have a name. Later, when she attended New Point School, grades one through high school were taught. It wasn't the building most of us remember them tearing down to build the firehouse. The original building had burnt and a second one with a large auditorium erected. In September of 1939, New Point became an elementary school with consolidation of high schools. It closed altogether when the county consolidated all schools, segregation coming to an end.

Helen Hurst said the office had no boxes so the customers had to get the mail while she was on duty. It hadn't presented a problem, since the waterman usually arrived home by noon. Many, like Stuart Harris, who faithfully walked to the post office every day to take down the flag, are retired. Family units are still close enough for relatives to pick up the mail of those, who are not able to do so, during the officer's hours.

"Lots of people still think of it as a meeting place. They come to sit and talk. Why I've got one lady who usually comes for an hour every day," commented Mrs. Hurst.

In 1988, Marion Grey Trusch, who calls herself the mayor of Bavon, and her mother, Mrs. Norman Burroughs, had their picture taken while collecting their mail from the OIC, Mary Alice Hudgins, for another *Gloucester-Mathews Gazette Journal* article. The article stated that there is no question that the location of the small Bavon Post Office had played a key role in the survival of a friendly community. "Described as clannish and fiercely loyal to that part of the county they call home, Bavon residents draw their strength from daily visits to the post office. Bavon Post Office is the place where neighbors meet to exchange tidbits of information, where news of births, deaths and other significant milestones are discussed. On the bulletin board in the post office, patrons post items for sale, church notices, and other news clippings. Magazines and coupons are exchanged, arts and crafts are proudly displayed and homemade cookies and candies are shared."

The article stated: "Today, Bavon serves 50 families with general delivery and 33 families on Star Route. Describing her job as more than 'just handing out mail,' Mrs. Hudgins says she feels very close to the patrons of Bavon.

"'Sometimes the bench is full of people,' she said, pointing to a wooden bench sitting near a sidewall. 'You find out who's sick, the latest news, politics, and recipes. Most of the people here are older and I find their stories interesting.'"

The doors closed on Bavon Post Office in January 1993, when Ruth Ann Ray was the OIC. The mail went to Port Haywood with the majority of the patrons receiving their mail by highway carrier on the Star Route.

In fact, Mrs. Trusch now owns the property where the store and post office operated, purchasing it for the purpose of preservation after the post office closed. In our second telephone conversation, she spoke in high regard of her treasured building that looks like a museum from the window displays. She has hosted neighborhood meetings in the closed post office. Mrs. Trusch said that she had to install shutters to hide the mail chute after she found people had deposited mail.

"I was going to write a letter,

But a postal card is better,

So please accept this friendly little rhyme:

It's not so pretty,

And it's not so witty,

But it shows I don't forget you all the time."

Post Card 1916

Bavon Post Office 1980s

Zip Code Enhances Mail Service

When I first heard that all mail would require zip codes in early 1963, I feared I wouldn't always know the correct code to place on an envelope. Or would I forget my own zip code? My husband and I operated a small business and had just moved the retail store with my drapery and slipcover workrooms into a building at Mathews Court House, transporting fabrics and machines in a snowstorm on April 1, 1963. Zip codes became effective in July 1963. Soon I received notice that for a small fee, I could obtain a book with all zip codes in the United States. I grabbed at the opportunity and use the paperback edition until this day.

I had understood in 1963 that the new system would make our mail more efficient so didn't question our leaders in the field. However, research has taught me that after catalogs and parcel post became popular, mail increased constantly. So in the early 1900s, the Post Office Department had looked at crude sorting machines after they introduced the canceling machines. Nothing materialized before the Great Depression. Then World War II put everything on hold except war related items. It wasn't until 1959 that they successfully tested a letter-sorting machine. Though the system wasn't perfect by 1963, enough had been established in the central post offices to initiate the use of a bar code from each zip code.

What did the system with five numbers tell post office employees? ZIP is an abbreviation for "Zoning Improvement Plan." The first digit designated a broad geographical area in the United States, ranging from "0" in the Northeast to "9" in the far West. The next two digits designated sectional centers accessible to common transportation networks, located in heavily populated areas. The final two digits pinpointed small post offices or zones in larger zoned cities. (Gleaned from *History of the United States Postal Service*)

Some of us wondered if it would work. Norman B. Rorher, founder of the "Christian Writers Guild," attended Evangelical Press Convention in Philadelphia after the system went into effect. He sent himself a post card to Norm Rorher, 91011 (ZIP Code for LaCanada, California.). "It beat me home," Rorher explained.

Marguerite Sadler, postmaster at Moon, had explained the system to her three grandsons, who resided in Hawaii, where their father was stationed with an Army assignment, when the system went into effect. One said they were going to test Grammie's postal system. He addressed a post card to "Grammie, 23119." He signed his name on the message side, and she received it in a few days after it was cancelled.

By 1967, the Post Office required mailers of second- and third-class bulk mail to presort by ZIP Code. The public and mailers adapted well, but it was not enough. Therefore, the agency added four more numbers in 1983. The sixth and seventh numbers denote a delivery sector while the last two denote a delivery segment, which in our case denotes a group of post office boxes or a road intersecting other roads and the family's box.

By the end of 1984, they had installed 252 optical character readers (OCRs) in 118 major processing centers across the country. These readers processed 24,000 pieces of mail per hour—a substantial increase compared to the 1,750 per work hour by the former machines.

Today they have a more high-powered reader that reads and bar codes nine or more per second. However, the remote bar-coding machine has to be used for handwritten script mail. Mathews County residents if you read this section carefully, you know why your mail has to go to Richmond when it's for another post office in the county. With today's overflow, it would take longer and more workers to sort it all in Mathews Post office as in days gone by.

With all the new machines, the Postal Service had lost and was losing money in the early nineties. Fax machines and email reduced first class mail tremendously. The deficit finally reached over $2 billion. However, they downsized small post offices, trimmed overhead positions, and offered early-out retirements and other incentives. The Postal Service no longer offers third class mail and postage has increased. The deficit has been reduced considerably—I could not find if any deficit remained. Mail is a part of our lifestyle, the post office still serving an important role.

I have observed that companies, who need your address for mailing you products shown on the web sites, need to update their electronic equipment. They seldom allow the last four digits of the ZIP Code.

With the introduction of the ZIP code, the Postal Service introduced two-letter-capital abbreviations for all states. For instance in the past, you simply put Mathews, and the state. You had two popular choices: Virginia or Va.

However, today I now write Mathews, VA 23109-0898 for my address. But remember, the only time you write abbreviations for states in this manner; a ZIP code follows. (Janet A. Fast reminded her readers of this in a *Chesapeake Style* editorial in 2002)

Although personal mail has decreased with the use of the Internet, telephones in every home and cell phones, my sister and I help keep letters in the mail. She uses standard large notebook paper and asks that I do the same so as not to crowd my writing. We write four to five pages on both sides weekly except when something unusual prevents us. Then we have a 20 or 30-minute phone conversation, which is nice once in a while. This way, though we are over 400 miles apart, we stay closely bonded. Pictures and other inserts in many of our letters add to the postage; but we want to keep the mails both flying by air and rolling to our mailboxes so we can stay in contact. We both do this in our down time in the evenings. I often remember I'm behind on journaling, but my sister has all that should be in my journal. I even express many of my inward feelings to her in my letters.

"It isn't how much you know, it's what you do with what you know." John Hunter

Chapter Ten

"Terms Cash—A boy at a crossing having begged something of a gentleman, the latter told him that he would give him something as he came back. The boy replied: 'You would be surprised if you knew how much money I loose by giving credit in that manner." The Richardson Review *November 1927*

Mail Carriers

As stated in the first of the book, most mail came by boat in the earlier years. But in the 1800s, when the first post offices were established in the county, carriers traveled to and from Gloucester Post Office by horse and a conveyance of one type or another, transporting overland mail. Little more than a century later, with the use of horseless carriages and the ferry crossing York River from Gloucester Point to Yorktown and back, there were two points to obtain and deliver Mathews County's ground mail since some came to Lee Hall train depot. Sometimes the same carrier ran both routes with a hired man to do one. In other years, USPS found it more economical to use two carriers. Seekers of a route submitted bids so the lower bidder won. Other carriers picked up and delivered mail within the county. Today, once the mail has reached the major mail-processing center in our area, which in our case is Richmond, Virginia, trucks bring the mail from there to Mathews Post Office and other offices on the route, picking up the outgoing mail. They make two trips a day to and from the county daily except Sunday.

My family met an automobile with the USPS insignia on the sides when coming home from Gloucester on a Sunday during the 2004 Christmas season. I asked, "What's that, Special Delivery?" "Yes, and though the charge is steep, the post office will lose money on that delivery," my son Wade replied. We knew the carrier had driven approximately 90 miles from Richmond and was returning— 180 miles round trip.

Three or more local carriers pick up their containers at Mathews Post Office to deliver mail to their designated post offices and Star Routes, returning with any outgoing mail. The Old Chesapeake Township Route has become too much for one driver with many more home deliveries on the Star Route so she has an assistant. Since I live on the route, I've learned Gerald Jones, the former North postmaster, covers it many days. Substitutes work in case of sickness or vacations.

I have been able to access minimal information, concerning who those brave men and women were by name in the nineteenth and early twentieth centuries. But I want to pay tribute to all, whether their names appear here or not. Richard Billups, whose contract is shown in Chapter One, was Mathews County's first official mail carrier. Other names do not appear in public records during the nineteenth century. And I only located a portion of the mail carriers, who carried out the service in Mathews County during the twentieth century.

On March 21, 1912, the following appeared in the *Mathews Journal*: "Mr. Frank Blassingham, the mail carrier from upper Mathews, was recently kicked by a horse and has not been able to attend to his duties."

The *Mathews Journal* gave this news item on July 3, 1913: "After having carried the mail for more years than are remembered by the younger inhabitants, Mr. E. T. Forrest has retired to private life and Mr. Harry Hammond will carry the mail in the future. Uncle 'Tom,' as he was familiarly known, had become a fixture and we will miss his daily visits to our city. The Gloucester route also changed hands, being now carried by Mr. E. M. Blake. J. J. White held the contract during the last four years."

Thomas Hunley, Jr. remembers when Todd Christian ran a bus service to Lee Hall Railroad Depot, picking up and delivering mail daily for the county as he transported passengers. Anne H. Davis told about her uncle, Howard A. Sadler, bidding for the Gloucester Route in or about 1926. Having the winning bid, he transported the mail to and from Gloucester for Mathews County for a number of years. It seems these two runs may have overlapped from the available information.

While performing his service to and from Gloucester, Howard Sadler placed a bid for the local carrier to Fitchetts, Diggs, Moon, and Tabernacle from Mathews Post Office. He received the contract, and George Owens usually drove the route. Sadler lived in Field Neck on Fitchetts Wharf Road. So we elementary school children near Fitchetts Post Office rejoiced because George Owens, with Sadler's permission, let us pile in the back of the stake-backed truck with a tarpaulin covering it, and ride with the mail bags the two or more miles to Milford Haven School mornings. After the driver let us off, the truck kept on to Diggs Post Office.

While visiting my cousin, the former Miss Elizabeth Gwynn, in Norfolk in July 2000, her younger sister joined us for lunch at the Norfolk Naval Base area. I had some of my articles that had been published in *Chesapeake Style* for Elizabeth to read. They had lived at Fitchetts with their parents at the grandparents' home in earlier days. In a conversation about our early school years when we rode in the back of the mail truck, her sister told about the day she stood too near the back wheel of the truck when it left. So it ran over her foot. The Stanley Owens family lived across the road from the school. Mrs. Estelle Owens heard a scream and came running. She took the child into her house, laying her on the kitchen table to access the damage. The kind-hearted lady administered something to the bruised foot for cleansing—probably turpentine. Sister said she fell asleep on the table, awakening in the afternoon. Estelle had evidentially given her something by mouth for pain. The girl left with a limp and did little walking for some days.

Howard A. Sadler married my mother's sister, Marguerite Richardson, and their house sat some yards towards Fitchetts on the opposite side of the road from ours—both with lanes. Their parents arrived yearly on Christmas Eve so the sisters rotated serving Christmas dinner from year to year. It was always at least one o'clock before either household was prepared to eat. I vividly remember the Christmas when Uncle Howard told Momma not to feel bad if he slipped away a bit before he finished eating. One child on his mail route had no Santa Claus that morning because Santa was delivering the toy he wanted by mail. (In those days, Santa delivered little more than some fruit, hard candy and maybe nuts in a well-worn-clean cotton stocking, one toy and new clothing if there was enough cash). The truck would be in Mathews at two o'clock on that day with any undelivered packages that had come. He slipped away before he emptied his plate or had dessert. After he left, my aunt commented on what she called his pledge: "Neither snow nor rain nor heat nor gloom of night stays these couriers from the swift completion of their appointed rounds." I felt proud that my uncle took such responsibility. In less than an hour, Uncle Howard returned, finishing his plate of food and joining us for dessert. He was smiling. "It was worth my effort to see that child's face glow."

Dewey Wroten made the run to Gloucester for some years after Sadler. Mrs. Marjorie Wroten said when I interviewed her that her father-in-law, Dewey Wroten, often did two runs a day--one to Lee Hall and one to Gloucester.

John W. Dixon, whose two grandfathers, Dillehay and Dixon, served as postmasters, described Wroten vividly in an email: "Mr. Wroten was a very friendly and accommodating person who would give a citizen a ride on his truck while transporting the mail. I have fond memories of him and the truck. On duty, he always wore his gun, which was required by the Post Office Service to command respect from postmasters and other contacts and to protect the mail. As a boy of eleven or twelve years of age, I rode with the mail from Hudgins to Gloucester Court House on a number of occasions. Whether or not my grandfather approved and arranged the rides is not known, but there seemed to be no restriction when my friends and I wanted to go. My friend Bud Dunton and I were in bicycle repair business, and as such, traveled to Gloucester to shop at 'Western Auto' store for repair parts. My Uncle John Dillehay and another friend Loyld Smith, who also repaired bikes at Redart, occasionally traveled with us. So when parts were needed, we rode the truck to Gloucester where upon arrival we would have about an hour to do our shopping. We rode with the mailbags under the tarpaulin, which covered the rear of Mr. Wroten's stake-bodied truck. On the ride to and from Gloucester, the truck briefly stopped at all of the in-between post offices for delivery and pickup of the mailbags and packages. On our return trip, the favorite stop was James Store, the halfway point on the mail run. It was here on hot days that Mr. Wroten would buy each of us a Pepsi Cola®, 12 ounces for a nickel; as the bottle deposit was two cents, we had to finish the Pepsi before departing— we could not delay the mail. Apparently our parents were not concerned about our all day excursions with Mr. Wroten. Perhaps they were glad to have us gone and in safe hands. No one knew if Mr. Wroten's gun was loaded or if it would fire."

If the reader is too young to understand "deposits on bottles," our soft drinks came in glass bottles. Therefore the storekeeper paid two cents for each bottle when he stocked the sodas. The company's truck driver picked up the empty bottles when he delivered drinks. If the storekeeper was short a bottle, he had to pay two cents extra. The bottling company sterilized the bottles, reusing them with new pry-off caps. When the lip of the bottle became chipped, the companies continued to use them as long as they'd seal. I often lost my two cents in the latter years of such containers, throwing the bottle away for fear someone would cut their lip on the ragged edge. Few throwaway items existed in those days. "A penny saved is a penny earned," first penned by Benjamin Franklin, was the motto.

John Wesley Wroten, Dewey's son, drove the Gloucester route for his father when he reached proper age. In one interview, the resident felt John Wesley drove the route a long time. But his widow, Mrs. Marjorie Wroten, said that he drove for his father when needed.

Gene Phillips wrote an article for *The Daily Press,* Newport News, Virginia, about Archie T. Hudgins of Port Haywood when he retired in 1960. I gleaned the following information about Archie's service from it. Hudgins nephew's wife, Anne Williams Hudgins, formerly of Mathews County, near where I grew up, mailed me the article after she talked with me on the phone.

Hudgins worked until age 65, after 35 years as mail carrier in Mathews County. He had used several methods of delivering the mail—horseback, horse and buggy, a horse-drawn sleigh, auto and truck. He received his first contract in 1925 before the county had hard surfaced roads.

In his earlier years of service with the Postal System, Hudgins had met a steamboat that brought the mail to the county, and then made his rounds. At that date, he only served four post offices, and only three families received their mail in boxes at their gates. After the 1930s, he picked the mail up at Mathews Post Office. And when he retired, the route covered a larger portion of the county with 16 post offices and 126 families on his Star Route.

Hudgins traveled a ten-mile distance to deliver mail in 1925, but upon retirement it had grown to 55 miles. Even though the miles grew, his workday had become shorter than in earlier years. Trucks traveled faster than his horse had. Back then, he left home at 7 a.m. and returned about 2:30

p.m. in contrast to the latter years when he worked nine to two. It was in those earlier years that the county suffered severe cold winters with snow on the ground and roads for a month at the time. The surface would melt in the sun, freezing over at night. This made the roads like packed ice. And he wasn't traveling in Alaska! He usually used a buggy, but had to resort to the sleigh during the extreme weather after a blizzard or deep snow.

Hudgins was born at Laban and married Eleanor Williams of Port Haywood, residing near his wife's home after marriage. The couple had one son, Judson, who eventually settled in Newport News where his work was located.

In a telephone conversation, an experience Anne had heard about Archie's service concerned how terrible his car usually looked after traveling the dirt roads with dust flying or mud spattering its sides. It actually had rows of muck on it. After he arrived home one sunny day, Eleanor got a bucket of sudsy water and a brush and washed the car, polishing it fit for a parade. The next day a storm came up before he finished his route. So when he arrived home, he was a bit ashamed of the new rows of mud on the car—"but it couldn't be helped," he told Eleanor.

Hudgins looked forward to just working his land, taking care of his livestock, and oystering on the day of his retirement. He lived until 1963, enjoying the work he had learned as a boy. But his former customers still remember Archie T. Hudgins and the service he gave.

When Norma Haislip Ashburn and I talked, I learned she grew up in post offices since her grandmother, Linda Steger, and her mother, Mary Steger Haislip, both served as postmasters, covering Foster, Bohannon and Mobjack offices either as postmasters or assistants. She took high school courses with the same profession as her goal. But that changed with the introduction of computers in the post offices so she studied home nursing. But her younger years, living in the north end of Mathews County and going to work with her mother or sometimes grandmother, acquainted her with mail carriers both from Gloucester and Lee Hall routes and with the local carriers that served Whites Neck.

Ashburn's grandfather, Martin Lewis served as the second postmaster at Mobjack Post Office. In the 1930s, Lewis won the contract for carrying mail in West and North Mathews. Ashburn noted by the early 1950s mail was delivered twice daily. She didn't know how many years the service continued. My research proves at the larger post offices, it continues today.

Norma Ashburn remembered John Wesley Wroten delivering the mail. As noted earlier, he worked for his father, Dewey Wroten. Her memories of last names of mail carriers through the years are: Mrs. Ward, Mr. German, and Arthur Hudgins from Gwynns Island, whose wife traveled with him. Then she remembered Irvy Milton Hudgins, known as Mike, whose wife Josephine sometimes traveled with him. Rev. Frank Seal, who had directed a Boys' Home near Dutton Post Office, received an appointment. Seal wasn't too well so his wife Ruth, traveled with him at times. After his death, Ruth acquired the route and continues to deliver the mail today. The Seals' daughters assisted when necessary, especially during their father's illness.

Labin Lee Hudgins, known in the county as "Leb," worked long past most folk's retirement at 65. Retiring in June 1977 at age 74, he knew he had carried the mail about 50 years—couldn't remember just when he began according to a *Gloucester-Mathews Gazette-Journal* reporter. In the early years of his service, "Leb" Hudgins drove a horse and buggy, delivering mail from the Onemo area to Mathews Court House. Before his retirement, he covered all points east and west of Mathews Court House, driving his small truck.

Older customers spoke highly concerning "Leb" Hudgins' service. If he ever missed a letter, he drove back to the mailbox to deliver it. If a package were too large for the mailbox, he would blow the horn on his pickup until someone came from the house to pick it up.

"'Leb' not only carried mail, but also did postal favors for people along his route. For some years during his service, he also delivered eggs to patrons on his route—a sideline for he and his sister, with whom he lived." (Facts from *Gloucester-Mathews Gazette-Journal* June 1977)

From the article that the above refers, our local paper published June 6, 1977 reads: "In later years, when his route served the entire Winter Harbor area including Onemo, Diggs and old Laban Post Office and down into New Point, 'I served over 200 boxes,' he said. 'I carried mail for Arthur Hudgins, Pres Forrest, Henry Diggs. What else do you want to know?'

"Hudgins didn't find much of his career noteworthy. Apparently the job came so naturally to him that he considered the extras all in the line of duty. His sister, Mrs. R. L. Callis, put his career in a different light.

"'He waited on them hand and foot,' she said. 'It's a hard job. Some days there wasn't much and others there were whole big bags. He has a lots of friends.'"

Folks missed seeing him in his red truck, giving all motorists a sociable greeting with a one-finger wave from the pickup's wheel. After the years of traveling the roads whether sick or well, "Leb" enjoyed summers in his garden and winters by the stove and visiting neighbors. He lived to age 81. "Leb" lived in the neighborhood where my husband and I built our home.

Today the three official mail carriers in the county are: Ruth Seal, Patricia Smith and Shelia Becker.

"Last week I stated that this was the ugliest woman I had ever seen. I have since been visited by her sister and now wish to withdraw that statement." Mark Twain

Post Cards

"Don't you think it's your turn to Write?"
Post Card 1916

The Postal Service issued postal cards first on May 1, 1873, and privately manufactured postcards became available soon afterwards. The first large distribution of the latter took place at the Columbian Exposition in Chicago in 1893. One had to squeeze a message on the side of the picture or on the end of the addressed side during the first printings. But the government allowed the back of the card to be divided into two sections in 1907, giving space for a short message. It cost a penny to mail postcards from 1899 until 1953 when the postage doubled. Today one pays 23 cents for a postage stamp for a postcard.

When I inherited my husband, Kirby's Aunt Irene Brooks' postcards, I didn't think too much about what they may mean to family history in the future. But I've learned that they reveal much about her life from the early teen years on until about 15 years before her retirement.

According to the family, Irene had attended Woodland School through the sixth grade. She walked six miles from Garden Creek, now Bashi Shores, to and from school. Upon completing Woodland School, Irene needed to continue her education if she was to teach. So Irene's father, Edward Kirby Brooks, known as Kirby, let her move to Portsmouth, Virginia to attend high school. He had a first cousin there with a daughter about Irene's age, Otherwise, she'd have to board with strangers in Mathews Court House area. Postcards with pictures of sites in the city intrigued Irene and made an easy way to update Mama and Papa about her progress. "CIB," as she signed her correspondence from her early teens, also sent postcards home on special occasions. Her mother started Irene's collection with the ones that she sent from Portsmouth. Of course, Irene spent summers at home on Garden Creek with her cousin, Ruth Stores, visiting the farm.

The messages related in a few words how pleased she was with the school system, showing no signs of homesickness. There are cards that she sent to her younger brother, Elwood, asking him to write. His February cards read: "My Valentine..." signing them "Very, very much sincerely, CIB."

The postcards, which I've found, dating one year after her stay in Portsmouth were sent to her at State Normal School, Harrisonburg, Virginia. However, there are postcards addressed to Irene during the summers of the years during State Normal School to other areas of Mathews County than her home address. She taught or did student teaching at Peninsula School, Bohannon, boarding with a resident, after her first year at the school, according to cancellation dates. A student named Lena Owens from Bohannon sent a post card, saying with thanks that she had received her certificate in June of 1913. Other cards were sent to Hudgins, appearing to make reference to the fact that she was teaching colored disabled children during a summer. "Colored" was written on the face of the cards, advertising the course Hampton Institute sponsored. It appeared Irene gave the cards to those who mailed them.

Irene attended four years of college, graduating from the University of Virginia with a B.S. degree in Library Science. Yet there are few postcards in the batch either sent by or to Irene while she lived in Charlottesville, Virginia.

She served as librarian in a school in Goochland County, receiving mail at Tabscott Post Office, early in her career. She'd stay in one county until she tired of it, moving on for a better salary or change of scenery. There are cards to Burdette, Virginia, and Rochelle, Virginia among others.

Irene and her two close friends, Sophie and Eddie, who attended the University of Virginia with her, made pact a "to be friends always." They agreed to take trips to the places that they had talked and longed to go. The postcards show a European trip was the first with pictures of castles and the snow-capped Alps. They attended the New York World's Fair and lastly drove across the United States, taking a northern route and coming home through the south.

After a time, Sophie married a North Carolina chicken farmer, but she made the trip across country some years after she married. Sophie and her husband lived in a large home on "Carrollton Chicken Farm" in the western part of the state. Although one postcard shows an oval picture of Irene, Sophie and Eddie on left side of the face of the card, displaying a "Carrollton" flag-like banner in the center of the right side. Above the flag at the very top, it reads: "Fine chickens always." Below the flag at the lower edge, it asks but with a period, "How do you like these." It appears Sophie's husband had a bit of humor for one wonders does he refer to the attractive women in long dresses or his chickens?

Irene's postcards prove that next to her home at Onemo, she enjoyed her visits to "Carrollton Farm" most. In her working years, she spent many Thanksgivings and a bit of her summer vacations with Sophie. Eddie joined them when possible.

In the late thirties, Irene's mother became confined to bed with rheumatoid arthritis. It became necessary that Irene stay home to help Papa. Mathews Memorial Library had need for a librarian so she accepted the opening, staying in the county for a time after her mother's death. However, she was ready to go back into the school system so found work in the state's rural high schools. The pupils, and perhaps some teachers, remembered her during Christmas and summer vacation with postcards. When her father became unable to care for himself, he spent a time before his hospitalization with his son and family. In 1946, they became my in-laws, Elwood and Edith Brooks. Their youngest son, Justin, was still in grammar school and Elwood Kirby, Jr., whom I later married, fighting in the Pacific Arena during Kirby Brooks' stay in the home.

After her Papa's death, Irene worked as high school librarian in Melbourne, Florida. It was in the mid forties and she enjoyed it for a time, but she missed Christmas with the family or spent a good bit of the holiday break traveling. Thanksgiving, she made it only as far as North Carolina to Sophie's farm for a short visit.

Postcards told what telephone calls, emails and notes do today. Hers seemed to have ceased in the late fifties. She sent and received letters or phone calls. Irene retired at the home where she was born in 1971, living her last twelve years in the county. She enjoyed living in the farmhouse, dating back to her grandparents, Rienza and Cotha Minter Brooks on Garden Creek.

Some greetings and messages used extensively in both Irene's postcards from local folks and others that have been loaned me, I find amusing are: "Heighho," "have a dandy time," and "have a fine time."

Scott Sadler loaned me his collection of postcards. He found them in the attic of the home that his great-great grandfather, Anthony Hudgins, had built before the family sold it. Among them I found cards, commemorating the Jamestown Exposition in 1907. This affair honored the 300th year since Jamestown was settled and took place at the Naval Base, Norfolk, Virginia. They depict the Machinery and Transportation Building, the fine homes that the states built in brick, advertisement of the event with John Smith's and President Theodore Roosevelt's pictures, United States Government Pier and the U. S. Life Saving Station all in full color. A black and white card shows the "Interior view of The Old Virginia Shoe Shop," stating it's *Craddock-Terry Co.'s* exhibit. And "The Smallest Man in the South" poses for the camera on a second black and white card, advertising the *Largest Shoe Manufacturers* of the *South*, an ad for the above company. Regarding the photo, a message explained that Col. A. I. Sawyer, of Key West, Florida, was a little more than 40 years old, 41 inches high and weighed 48 pounds. Sawyer advertised Craddock-Terry's shoes because they are "Long wear Shoes." The shoes wear so well that the company had to build multiple factories in Lynchburg, Virginia, shipping them far and near. These postcards only had space for the address and the senders name and address on the backside. However, some wrote over the pictures while others wrote on the end of the addressed side.

My husband, Kirby, made regular bi- monthly trips to Richmond, buying supplies for our business through the years. To offset traveling costs, he usually loaded the truck with used newspapers, magazines and other paper products to sell for recycling. I don't think any traveling cost came out of that money except his lunch, but gave him money to have on hand for emergencies or my Christmas gift. In those days, few had heard of the term "recycle" so popular today. Therefore people gladly handed over the stacks of newspapers, magazines and whatever paper products they had accumulated, saving them many hours of burning. It pleased the schools and county library to telephone for a free pickup of old books and periodicals rather than to hire someone to haul the items away. In some of these pickups, the postcards from a Gloucester estate happened to be in the group. Kirby was a worse packrat than I am, and that's saying a lot of stuff accumulated. Having to separate paper products into groups, he easily found the treasures. After his death, I found the postcards he'd accumulated neatly packed in a box. I have sold some and still have some. They dated from 1898 until the 1930s, telling of their travels. Mama or Grandmother had saved the treasured remembrances for the sender to keep on their return home.

None of the collections that I have viewed personally covered one town, city or state—just recorded the person's travels. However, the Dailey Press published an article by Patti Rosenburg on January 6, 2002, regarding collectors of Williamsburg postcards, whom she interviewed. I found it interesting enough to clip and save. A man from Maryland had near 3,000 postcards of scenes in Williamsburg. Many of places no longer exist. The ordinary postcards that I sold brought about 25 to 50 cents each in the late 1970s. Yet, I've learned since researching the subject some pay hundreds of dollars for a particular card, and a serious collector has been known to pay thousands of dollars for a coveted card. I went to www.williamsburgpostcards.com, finding that I could view thousands of cards, but they only show the display of Kris Preacher. There are no prices since they aren't for sale.

In the early twentieth century, Christmas Greetings, Valentines, Thanksgiving and Easter cards seemed to be mostly postcards with one-cent postage. They were the fad, but treasured enough that most were saved. Back then the card could cost much more than the postage, depending on the subject or artwork.

Postage Stamps

"I wonder where the letters go,
Round here there's been a dearth,
So I just thought I'd let you know."
(Anonymous)

We take so much for granted in the twenty-first century, including how we pay postage and apply it. There are many designs from which to choose in today's stick-on stamps. They are attached to a sheet of coated paper that allows one to remove the stamp and apply it directly to the envelope. Gone are the days of licking the raunchy glue coating or moistening the back of stamps with a sponge. Then companies and people with large amounts of outgoing mail choose to use metered mail with the postage stamped on the envelope or package.

According to the *Funk and Wagner Encyclopedia,* English schoolmaster Hill first suggested the idea for the adhesive stamp in 1837. Through Hill's efforts, on May 1, 1840, Great Britain released the worlds first officially issued adhesive postage stamp, a one-penny denomination universally referred to as the *Penny Black.* The stamp portrayed a picture of Queen Victoria, which established a postal precedent in Great Britain. Since that time, all regular-issue stamps in England have portrayed the reigning monarch.

According to" History of the United States Postal Service" web site, Congress passed a bill, approving gummed postage stamps March 3, 1847. The first sales took place in New York City on July 1, 1847. I find no mention of the face the stamp portrayed. However all the older stamps that I've found bear Government officials' pictures. Stamped envelopes came on the market in 1852. With the introduction of stamps and prepaid postage, the mail carrier had an easier day. When all mail came C.O.D., it became a bit of hassle to find the recipient at home if a man lived alone to accept and pay for the letter.

The United Postal Service web site reported that the first commemorative stamps pictured the *Columbian Exposition in 1893.* Postmaster General Wanamaker authorized them to consist of a series of 15 stamps with face value ranging from one cent to five dollars. Congress declared them "unnecessary" stamps since the two, three, four and five-dollar stamps would be more than any postage charge. The only way to use the full value of the five-dollar Columbian stamp would be to mail a 62-pound, eight-ounce package of books at book-rate class postage. However Wanamaker believed they would become moneymakers. History proved him correct. Two billion commemorative Columbian stamps were sold, amounting to over 40 million dollars. People stood in lines to buy their share. Wanamaker purchased 5,000 two-dollar stamps for $10,000, placing them in his safe as an investment. When he died, they remained where he placed them, but the value had increased to $22,500. A fad or new investment of stamp collecting had been started that continues into the twenty-first century.

Stars, artists, painters, doctors, nurses, inventors, judges, presidents, musicians and military leaders are among the many people depicted on United States stamps to date. Important expeditions, the moon landing and other historical events, including the 15 cloud formations that have been recorded, enhance either envelopes or collectors pages. I've recently learned one works to prove the worth of a person or event pictured on postage stamps before the stamp goes to press.

In 2004, Dr. Edwin (Ned) Logan is directing a project, which was initiated by the Williamsburg Stamp Society, and studied under the auspices of Jamestown 2007 Steering Committee of the Jamestown-Yorktown Foundation and its partners, proposing a postage stamp and three postal cachets by students to celebrate Jamestown's 400th Anniversary in 2007. If approved, the stamps and three caches will be sold at Jamestown Settlement and Historic Jamestowne during 2007.

In early 2006, Virginia's K-12 students, higher education visual arts and graphic students, and K-12 visual arts educators will be invited to submit entries for postal cachet designs—a design printed on the face of an envelope—for Jamestown's 400th anniversary. Three winning cachet designs will be chosen from the six categories submitted for the envelopes. This project has taken months of Dr. Logan's endeavors, and they still wait for the decision. So when you find a favorite postage stamp in the future, remember some group with a director has worked hard to give you the subject.

The Post Office Seal

"Beware of little expenses;
a small leak will sink a great ship."
Benjamin Franklin in *The Richardson Review* June 1927

According to the *History of the U.S. Postal Service*, Mercury originally symbolized the postal system in the United States." In 1782, Postmaster General Ebenezer Hazard used the figure of Mercury, the messenger of gods

and the god of commerce and travel in Roman mythology."
In 1837, Postmaster General Amos Kendall directed the seal
be changed to a circular insignia. It showed "a post horse in
speed, with mailbags and rider encircled by the words: Post
Office Department, United States of America." The latter is
believed to have been inspired by a crude woodcut circle that
Benjamin Franklin had issued on a circular letter when
Postmaster General.

On August 12, 1970, the Post Office Department
announced the adoption of a new seal. President Nixon also
signed the Postal Reorganization Act converting the Post
office Department into an independent establishment of the
executive branch. The seal featured a bald eagle poised for
flight on a white field, above red and blue bars framing the
words "U.S. Mail" and surrounded by a square border with
the words "United Postal Service" on three sides. Nine five-
pointed stars made the base of the insignia.

Mathews--a Unique County

Happy Homes and Fertile Farms On Smiling Water
Mathews County's Motto

From the earliest days in Mathews County, neighbors
not only knew each other, but everyone in the community
and those for miles around. Residents formed a bond through
attending church services together; meeting at the local
school socials and gathering at the general merchandise
stores. They may disagree or do things differently. Yet when
a stranger came in their midst, suggesting new life styles,
they stood together. All who gathered freight from the
nearest wharf soon became acquainted with folk from
surrounding communities.

I can't speak of too many men in the nineteenth
century. But I know my great uncles n the Richardson
genealogy left the County, traveling to Richmond and

213

Norfolk, Virginia, to find work, all establishing businesses in a few years except Uncle Raymond, who worked in the insurance business in his own company. However, their father and uncles had traveled the seas to make a living. One of Daddy's brothers became a sea captain and several cousins worked on the high seas. And I knew many in the county, who traveled on passenger and freight ships.

The County had its pastors, lawyers, doctors, dentists, bankers and merchants. Otherwise if a man didn't own a large farm, fishing, crab or oyster business, he went to sea. Daddy worked on freight ships, obtaining his quartermaster papers before he married. He, like others through the years, said you couldn't enter any port that wasn't familiar with Mathews County seamen.

Most residents, who have traveled in or out of the state, from Moon, Cobbs Creek, Onemo, Mobjack and other of the county's oddly named post offices have been questioned, "Where is that place?" In my own experience, living at Moon during my teen years, I had questions of all kinds tossed my way. Then when my husband and I moved to our home, we used Onemo Post Office. It's pronounced O-ne-mo,' but other places they say On'-e-mo among other pronunciations.

In early 2004, Rev. Thomas Steel, the pastor of Peniel Evangelical Friends Church, Onemo, found an interesting account of a letter reaching Richard Trusch, a resident at Laban and member of Peniel Church since its earlier days, though it had been addressed to Williams Wharf, Virginia. Trusch lived on Garden Creek and Williams Wharf sat on East River—over ten miles apart. My husband's grandfather, Rev. Wilbur C. Diggs, founder and pastor of Peniel Friends Church, had filed the paper and perhaps written it. A New York "drummer" had heard about the 7-year-old Trusch boy, whom a wealthy Mathews County farmer had adopted from the Norfolk orphanage. He knew a family in New York, who had migrated from

Germany through Norfolk. So he contacted them to see if they were related. Richard's sister wrote to the only address the "drummer" knew—Williams Wharf where his shipments went. The postmaster had heard of only one Trusch so sent the letter to Laban.

In time, Richard visited his family in New York, but returned to his home in Mathews County. He lived a Christian life, married and raised a family, moving near Laban Post Office, where he died in 1965 at age 83.

Mathews County has changed like the other parts of the country with increase in population and technology. Although the Mathews Court House and the folks on the main incoming highways didn't receive electricity until 1929 and other areas in 1939, we didn't know the difference until we had it to enjoy. It was the way all rural folk near us lived. All roads were dirt until 1930 when the state tarred the main highways. Some roads weren't hard surfaced until 1960 or later. Many farmlands have become small communities with homes on one or two acre lots. However, it remains a friendly community, most residents wave in passing whether they know you or not. On any day, residents that go to the post offices for mail or stamps stop to chat with a friend or former acquaintance. I've even met new residents, often called "come heres," in Mathews Post Office. New assistants come to work in the post office and often are promoted to their own post office in another section of the county as openings occur. Then another friendly face appears behind the counter.

Mathews County folks move at a slower pace than much of the country. Pastors in all denominations serve churches and come back to retire in some part of the county. Folks from all states come to visit, falling in love with the casual lifestyle. In a few years they have purchased a home or built a place for weekends and retirement. The United Parcel Service and American Express carriers stop in the business district, Mathews Court House, and while he delivers packages he finds where a few new customers live. Now that house numbers have been issued and roads named, he'll ask less often in 2005. The county has 35 churches open on Sundays though some have less attendance than in past years. Mathews County has been a great place to live during my lifetime. Even though with growth, I no longer know all my neighbors. I've enjoyed my walk through the necks and center of the county that Mildred P. Hudgins has called: "The place next to Heaven."

As you have read the statistics, remember I completed my research in December 2004. Postmasters may have changed and more post offices closed since that date. I've not included pictures of the current post office buildings. However, I do show pictures of the earlier location of the offices still open whether the office has moved or is in a new addition to the building. I regret pictures of some past post offices that are still open were not available.

Many articles from the Gloucester-*Mathews-Gazette-Journal* were found in the "Mathews County Historical Society's" archives. I had clipped and saved some articles just because they interested me so that saved hours of research.